THE CARDINAL'S COURT

THE CARDINAL'S COURT

The Impact of Thomas Wolsey in Star Chamber

J. A. GUY

Assistant keeper of Public Records at the Public Record Office; Former Fellow, Selwyn College, Cambridge; Visiting Lecturer, University of California, Berkeley (1977)

ROWMAN AND LITTLEFIELD

TOTOWA, NEW JERSEY

First published in the United States, 1977 by
ROWMAN AND LITTLEFIELD
81 Adams Drive, Totowa, New Jersey 07512

© 1977 J. A. Guy

ISBN 0–87471–815–5

Printed in Great Britain by
Redwood Burn Ltd, Trowbridge & Esher

Contents

Preface

This book arose out of a doctoral thesis submitted at the University of Cambridge in 1973. It is, however, a quite new study, and is more fully researched and more thoughtfully constructed than the thesis. In particular, it presents a more enlightened view of Wolsey's management of the Council, his conduct in Star Chamber, and the nature of early-Tudor conciliar jurisdiction. Nevertheless, the book could not have been written without the criticisms and enthusiasm of many scholars, notably Professor G. R. Elton (who supervised the thesis), Professor T. G. Barnes, Miss M. M. Condon, Dr. E. W. Ives, and Dr. J. H. Baker. I am deeply grateful for their advice and comment, while myself accepting full responsibility for the arguments and errors of the book. In addition, the extensive research required for both thesis and book could not have been completed without the exceptional facilities and support which I have enjoyed at many institutions. I am greatly in debt to the Master and Fellows of Selwyn College, Cambridge, and to Lord Lloyd; to the Public Record Office and its staff; and to the Director and staff of the Huntington Library, San Marino, California. I must also thank the Warden and Fellows of All Souls College, Oxford, and the staffs of the British Museum, the Folger Shakespeare Library, the

Bodleian Library, and the Cambridge University Library for research facilities. Chapter two of this book is a revised version of an article published in the *English Historical Review* in July 1976; I am grateful for permission to reproduce it here. Quotations from copyright documents in the Huntington Library and the Public Record Office appear by respective permissions of the Director and the Controller of H.M. Stationery Office. Finally, I wish to thank Mrs. D. P. Sherwood for typing the manuscript, and the staff of the Harvester Press for helpful suggestions.

The illustration on the jacket, which shows the *camera stellata*, is taken from the Foundation Indenture of Henry VII's Chapel (E33/2). Reproduction is by permission of the Controller of H.M. Stationery Office.

Cambridge, September 1976   J. A. G.

Abbreviations

Additional	B.M. Additional Manuscript
Bayne	*Select Cases in the Council of Henry VII,* ed. C. G. Bayne (London, Selden Society, 1958)
B.M.	British Museum
C.U.L.	Cambridge University Library
E.H.R.	*English Historical Review*
El	Henry E. Huntington Library, San Marino, California, Ellesmere Manuscript
Hargrave	B.M. Hargrave Manuscript
Harleian	B.M. Harleian Manuscript
Lansdowne	B.M. Lansdowne Manuscript
LP	*Letters and Papers, Foreign and Domestic, of the Reign of Henry VIII,* ed. J. S. Brewer, J. Gairdner, R. H. Brodie (London, 1862-1932)
P.R.O.	Public Record Office
St. Pap.	*State Papers during the Reign of Henry the Eighth* (London, Record Commission, 1830-52)
Stowe	B.M. Stowe Manuscript

Star Chamber records preserved at the P.R.O. are cited by the call number there in use without prefix:

1	(followed by bundle and piece numbers, e.g. 1/1/1)	Star Chamber Proceedings, Henry VII
2	(e.g. 2/1/1)	Star Chamber Proceedings, Henry VIII
3	(e.g. 3/1/1)	Star Chamber Proceedings, Edward VI
4	(e.g. 4/1/1)	Star Chamber Proceedings, Mary
10	(followed by bundle and piece numbers in the case of arranged documents, e.g. 10/1/1; followed by bundle number and part number of bundle in the case of unarranged material, e.g. 10/4, Pt. 2)	Star Chamber Proceedings, Miscellanea

Other manuscripts preserved at the P.R.O. are quoted by the full call number there in use. The descriptions of the principal classes referred to are as follows:

C 44	Chancery, Placita in Cancellaria, Tower Series
C 54	Chancery, Close Rolls
C 66	Chancery, Patent Rolls
C 82	Chancery, Warrants for the Great Seal, Series II
C 115	Chancery, Masters' Exhibits, Duchess of Norfolk Deeds
C 142	Chancery, Inquisitions Post Mortem, Series II
C 193	Chancery, Miscellaneous Books
C 244	Chancery, Files, Corpus Cum Causa
C 253	Chancery, Files, Sub Pena
C 254	Chancery, Files, Dedimus Potestatem
CP 40	Common Pleas, Plea Rolls

DL 3	Duchy of Lancaster, Depositions and Examinations, Series I
E 28	Exchequer, Treasury of the Receipt, Council and Privy Seal
E 36	Exch., Treasury of the Receipt, Miscellaneous Books
E 101	Exch., King's Remembrancer, Various Accounts
E 137	Exch., King's Remembrancer, Estreats
E 163	Exch., King's Remembrancer, Miscellanea
E 208	Exch., King's Remembrancer, Brevia Baronibus
E 315	Exch., Augmentation Office, Miscellaneous Books
E 401	Exch., Exchequer of Receipt, Enrolments and Registers of Receipts
E 405	Exch., Exchequer of Receipt, Rolls of Receipts and Issues
E 407	Exch., Exchequer of Receipt, Miscellanea
KB 27	King's Bench, Coram Rege Rolls
KB 29	King's Bench, Controlment Rolls
REQ 1	Court of Requests, Miscellaneous Books
REQ 2	Court of Requests, Proceedings
REQ 3	Court of Requests, Miscellanea
SP 1	State Papers, Henry VIII, General Series
SP 2	State Papers, Henry VIII, Folio Volumes
SP 60	State Papers, Ireland, Henry VIII

Figures in references to *LP* are to volumes and numbers of documents; in all other cases they are to pages. Where the original of a document calendared in *LP* has been used (almost always), the reference to the manuscript is given, followed by the reference to *LP*. In transcripts, abbreviations have been extended and modern punctuation has been adopted, with the result that capitals have occasionally been put where there is none in the original; otherwise, the spelling of the manuscript has been rendered exactly. In giving dates, the Old Style has been retained, but the year is assumed to have begun on 1 January.

1

Myth and Reality

MYTH AND COUNTERMYTH

The history of star chamber must be written from the court's extant records and those sources which throw light on records which are now missing.[1] Most previous work has proved deficient precisely because it has at best been founded on small samples of record material. The sheer formidableness of the thousands of sets of proceedings in the Public Record Office has discouraged systematic investigation of the court. Similarly, while historians have unanimously lamented the loss of the Henrician council registers, the series which continued after the creation of the privy council and its own registers as the star chamber order and decree books, few have made a real attempt to reconstruct the evidence that remains.[2] The Henrician court has in particular suffered misunderstandings arising from attempts to detect its origins. These efforts began in earnest as early as the reign of Elizabeth I. Record searching, followed by the compilation of books and treatises, was one manifestation of the strong interest in historical and antiquarian studies during the sixteenth and seventeenth centuries.[3] The aim common to star chamber enthusiasts was

1

to refute the popular myth that the court was erected in 1487 by Henry VII's so-called statute *'pro camera stellata',* and therefore possessed no legal authority except that derived from the act.[4] The writings of William Mill, William Lambarde and William Hudson claim some initial attention. All three wrote treatises after they had studied the early star chamber archive, and their work had a considerable influence on that of later historians.

The first contribution came in the form of a rough essay written in 1577 by Mill.[5] Perusal of the records had enabled him, as he thought, to perceive something of the origins of the court.

> Albeit that the Statute made Anno iij[tio] of King Henry the seventhe dothe authorise the Lord Chaunceller and certayne other persons to examin and punishe Ryottes, Rowetes and other misdemeanours mencioned in the same Acte. Yet it appearethe that the Authoritie and Jurisdiction of the Starre Chamber dothe not depende whollie uppon that Statute. For that the saied same Courte . . . is more aunciente then the saied Statute.[6]

It was apparent that 'divers Misdemeanours, Offences and other matters not mencioned in the saiede Statute have been harde and Judged in the Starre Chamber'.[7] Mill then turned his attention to the judges of the court. The registers showed that 'persons not named in the same Statute' had sat in star chamber: bishops, doctors and 'others' were to be discovered among the lists of the presence. This point perplexed Mill, who failed to see how non-members of the 'privy' council should attend at all.[8] He later added that the probability was that they were councillors of limited status: merely 'of that place' or 'at large'.[9] The lists of Henrician attendances also recorded the royal presence. Henry VII sat 'often', and Henry VIII 'in the beginning of his reign'.[10]

After Mill succeeded Thomas Marshe in the office of clerk of star chamber on 1 October 1587, the records of the court passed into his charge.[11] In 1590 the clerk composed 'A Discourse concerning the Antiquity of the Starrchamber occasioned by Certeyne Articles made by the Attourneys against the Courte and Clerke of the same'.[12] This treatise was Mill's rejoinder to the demands of Grimstone and Hexte, two dissident attorneys, who protested at the clerk's plans for the impending removal of the current records to a new star chamber office in the Holborn court of Gray's Inn.[13] The debate turned on whether the clerk enjoyed certain prescriptive rights by virtue of his office.[14] Mill took up the challenge and composed the treatise, drawing on his researches both in the star chamber archive and among the Tower records.[15] To the attorneys' suggestion that the court was erected by the act of 1487, Mill retorted: 'I doe know this to be an opinion ignorantly received of many yet approved of none that hath knowledge of the Court'.[16] The clerk then proceeded to equate the early court with the activity of the king's council, undifferentiated in its executive and judicial function until about the reign of Edward VI. The council chamber of the king, from the earliest times, was the forum for discussion of 'all matters of state', and 'all matters of mis-demeanours falling out between party and party'.[17] The theory implicit in Mill's writings was that the statute of 1487 served only to strengthen the power of the king's council sitting as a court. This was the meaning of his statement of 1577 that the jurisdiction of star chamber did not depend 'wholly' upon the act. As Mill wrote in his *Liber Intrationum,* 'the court was authorised' by the statute to 'reform' the offences which it rehearsed;[18] or, as a modern historian put the point, to an-nounce to offenders that 'another and very vigorous attempt would be made to crush out certain crying evils which were of long standing'.[19] This erroneous interpretation was fully worked out by William Lambarde.

Lambarde's first commentary on star chamber was prepared in 1586.[20] But this version was heavily revised in 1589, when the work was entitled 'Of the Courte called the Starre Chambre'.[21] With the clerk's assistance, Lambarde had gained access to the star chamber records, and a tribute is paid in the 1589 manuscript 'to William Mille, myne auncient favourer'.[22] Lambarde showed his work to Mill after its com-pletion, and the clerk referred to its contents in his own treatise of 1590.[23] On the origins of the court, Lambarde reached similar conclusions to Mill. The early star chamber was 'the ordinarie Counseil Chambre of the king when soever he and his Courte did lye and soiourne at his Pallaice in Westminster, frequented no lesse for deliberation upon matters of Estate, then for decreeing extraordinarie suites and causes of complaint'.[24] On the effect of the statute of 1487 in the Henrician period:

> . . . bothe king Henry 7 and king Henry 8 dyd (many yeares after the making of this Statute) sometymes in person, and verie often by their Counseil, practise that former Jurisdiction in the Starre Chambre, without any helpe of this new Lawe and Statute, it doth most certeinly appeare by the booke of Entries kept theare, which is a true Ephemeris (or Journale) of the Actes of that Courte.[25]

Lambarde considered that the 'ancient' jurisdiction of the medieval king's council was not subjected to statutory interruption. The status of the act of 1487 was to 'enlarge' the judicial competence of the council in respect of certain specified offences.[26] The statute therefore gave the court a 'new' or 'double' authority.[27] Its main purpose, and that of the supplementary act of 1529,[28] was to reconcile legal opinion to the punishment of misdemeanour by the king's ministers after the sworn examination of defendants and witnesses, and without trial at law as demanded by Magna Carta. Every aspect of the jurisdiction exercised in the Henrician period by the king's council was done by 'that former authority which they had'; but after 1487 the circumstances of these proceedings, namely venue, process and judges, enjoyed statutory sanction. Of the several attempts to reconcile star chamber with the tribunal named in the so-called act '*pro camera stellata*', Lambarde's was the most satisfying, and his exposition soon enjoyed wide acceptance.[29]

William Hudson's 'Treatise concerning the Court of Star Chamber' was a more scholarly enterprise than its predecessors.[30] The original version of the work was probably written between 1618 and 1621, and the final text was polished in the early years of the reign of Charles I.[31] Structurally the treatise was divided into three parts, each of which contained several considerations. The first part concerned the court itself. The second part examined the jurisdiction of star chamber and the cases heard there. The third described the procedure of the court. Hudson was not prepared to devote too much space to a discussion of origins. That star chamber was established by the statute of 1487 was 'a dotinge which noe man that had looked uppon the Recordes of the Courte would have lighted uppon'.[32] The court 'subsisteth by ancient prescription, and hath neither essence nor existance by that Act of Parliament'.[33] Its origins were rather to be detected in Henry II's reign.[34] On the judges of star chamber, the statute was equally irrelevant.[35] The judges were the king's councillors, and in the Henrician period the 'express' name of the court was 'the king's Council in the Star Chamber'.[36] The attendance of councillors in the reigns of Henry VII and VIII had been 'well near forty at some one time', and 'the court was most commonly frequented by seven or eight bishops and prelates every sitting day'.[37] This was a great advance on Mill's anachronistic theory of 'privy' councillors and councillors 'at large'. Hudson's account of the Henrician court's jurisdiction was, however, less satisfactory. The considerations of public, civil and criminal cases were weakened by the author's failure to distinguish correctly the judicial from the administrative *acta* of the council in the period before 1540 when both were recorded in the same series of undifferentiated registers. As a result, Hudson had the Henrician star chamber debating treaties, discussing commercial policies, receiving foreign ambassadors, and supervising the swearing-in of justices of the peace.[38] Historians who subsequently followed his analysis inevitably concluded that 'the Court of Star Chamber figured less as a judicial tribunal than as "the Council of State" – a title which it bore'.[39]

On star chamber litigation, Hudson offered some especially perceptive remarks. It is ironic that the most instructive of his statements has been given least credence by historians and lawyers: ' . . . there is noe man who hath at all looked into the ancient Records of this Court but doth well knowe that it is more Common in the tyme of Henry 7; and the beginning of the Raigne of Henry 8; that this Court examined, discussed and determined more Titles then Crimes.'[40] His ensuing discussion of the court's procedure was likewise methodical and historical. However, despite its length, it was heavily condensed and, because of its wide chronological scope, suffered from anachronisms in the interests of analytical coherence. It also contained such glaring errors as the statement that in Henry VIII's reign all examinations were taken before the lord chancellor in open court.[41] The 'Treatise' was nevertheless preferable to the writings of Mill and Lambarde. It was more substantial, more firmly based on the star chamber records, and less concerned with the abortive question of the court's antiquity.

THE MEDIEVAL BACKGROUND

Mill, Lambarde and Hudson were well guided in their historical outlook, even if their theories had often come close to establishing myths of a stature to rival that of the act 'pro camera stellata'. Star chamber did indeed inherit its jurisdiction by direct descent from the immemorial authority of medieval English kings and their councillors to redress grievances and adjudicate on the petitions of subjects.[42] From the fourteenth century onwards, the king's council met regularly enough in the camera stellata at Westminster and elsewhere, exercising the royal residuary powers delegated to it as need required and as time permitted. Judicial work was but one aspect of its activity: the council was always primarily a consultative, advisory and administrative body. Nevertheless, the steady continuity of a judicial role was a feature of the council's development. This was exemplified not least by the constancy of official contemporary reference to litigation 'coram consilio domini regis apud Westmonasterium in camera stellata', a description which was in use by 1392 and which persisted until 1641, the year of star chamber's statutory abolition.[43] Since the council was undifferentiated as to the executive and judicial areas of its operations, it enjoyed no specific organisation as a court; and although sometimes described by the word 'curia', this usage carried the full ambiguity that the 'court' of a medieval king in reality possessed. The council had no roll, seal or process pertaining exclusively to it.[44] It did not reserve set days for 'matters in law', although it might be said to be 'sitting judicially'.[45] Prior to the sixteenth century there was no concerted attempt by the council to manage its agenda or timetable its business, although its plenary sessions at Westminster were within the terms set for the king's courts.[46] The council was, however, well appointed for judicial work in its personnel. Those sworn or retained of the council included, in addition to the great men of the realm, the lords and knights, a specialist element in the presence of the chief and puisne justices, the barons of the exchequer, the sergeants-at-law and others *iusperiti in legem*.[47]

It was Edward I who had begun to mitigate the burden of examining the written petitions of his subjects by providing for an initial sorting by the chancellor and his staff.[48] By the reign of Edward III, the chancellor had acquired recognition as the servant of the king with responsibility for the expedition of the procedures of the council, within parliament or without.[49] Soon an unending stream of prayers and complaints, both written and oral, were addressed or referred to him.[50] As far as possible he would answer all requests himself, either by the issue of an original writ for an action at law, or by summoning the parties before him in chancery. However, those petitioners and others who had business of some importance were heard by the council.[51] Public order, administration, economic regulation and heresy were of notable concern.[52] In these areas the chancellor moved his conciliar colleagues, and cases would be taken into chancery *'ut tunc inde fiat quod consilio nostro videbitur faciendum'*.[53] The position had not changed in the reign of Richard II, when many suitors were addressing their petitions to the chancellor personally. A case of 1389 – the earliest extant example of a petition addressed to the chancellor followed by a decree – was heard *'coram consilio domini nostri Regis'* and judgment was pronounced *'per idem consilium'*.[54]

Under the Lancastrian kings the council was the seat of political power, administrative initiative and judicial policy. The period also saw substantial growth in the importance of the chancellor in government and justice.[55] The process had begun, and was completed under the Yorkists, which advanced the chancellor's position as a member and servant of the council dealing equitably with petitions to that of being head of an established, chancery court of equity.[56] But the eventual arrival of chancery as one of the four central courts of the realm, and the rise of the specialist courts of chivalry and admiralty, by no means relieved the council of its judicial responsibilities.[57] On the contrary the development of equity, which may have been accompanied by attempts to restrict the common-law side of chancery to cases of privilege and traverse, actively encouraged suitors to continue their ancient recourse to the council and to parliament, the latter being able to act effectively only through the council.[58] The records extant for the fifteenth century indicate the extent to which the council chamber was recognised as a forum for private litigation, especially that which could be set into a context of local disorder and subversion, perversion of justice and official maladministration.[59] Suitors were never slow to realise the potential offered by the council's willingness to proceed at once with both civil and criminal powers.[60]

Lancastrian policy and legislation also reinforced a tendency of the council to concentrate its law-enforcement function into the hands of the chancellor and the great officers of state, who exercised quasi-judicial, quasi-executive powers on behalf of the council, but outside its formal structure.[61] Such management of its affairs by the council was entirely in the interests of efficiency and economy. The chancellor and his associates did not conflict with the regular work of the council in the *camera stellata;* they complemented it in the areas specified by the statutes. The trend was, however, reversed at the Yorkist accession. Under the firm control of Edward IV, and especially after 1471, the council reabsorbed the range of its judicial work into the whole body.[62]

HENRY VII

By 1485 the traditions of conciliar government and justice were sufficiently well established in England to survive intact the cataclysmic political change which ensued upon the victory of Henry Tudor at Bosworth field. Moreover, the continuity was not merely one of tradition but also of personnel: out of forty of Edward IV's councillors who were still alive after 1485, twenty-two were councillors to Henry VII, notably John Morton, Thomas Rotheram and John Dynham; and twenty of Richard III's councillors served the new dynasty, of whom Rotheram and Dynham were again two.[63] Henry's council was also attended by fifteen close relatives of various Yorkist councillors, including the Bourchiers and Woodvilles. Others, such as Sir Richard Croft and Richard Empson, had similarly had careers under the Yorkists.[64] These men were added to the nucleus of a council which Henry had brought with him from exile in Brittany and France.[65] During the reign of Edward IV, one hundred and twenty-four persons bore the title 'councillor'.[66] For ,the reign of Henry VII, the names of two hundred and twenty-seven persons who attended the council have been discovered, mainly amongst lists of the presence which are extant for one hundred and thirty-five of its meetings.[67] These figures are undoubtedly minima. The exact totals will never be ascertained owing to the defective nature of the sources. Nor are the figures really comparable. The Ellesmere extracts provide evidence for Henry VII's council which is not available for that of Edward IV and which swells the ranks by noticing infrequent attenders in addition to the king's 'continual' councillors.[68] It is perhaps most meaningful to say that, at any one time, the early Tudor council may have numbered about seventy persons, of whom no more than forty or so could ever be got to meet. The usual presence at Henry VII's council ranged from seven to thirty persons.[69]

The composition of Henry's council was broadly traditional. The presence numbered the temporal lords, bishops and abbots, doctors of law and other lesser clerks, the knights of the household and other lay administrators, and the judges and lawyers from the chief justices downwards.[70] The trend, which became marked in the later years of Edward IV, towards the growing prominence of officials in the council was maintained under Henry VII.[71] The context for this was the king's demand for good and loyal service. The men 'regarded by the king as his most confidential and reliable councillors' were those who rose to fame – or infamy.[72] Henry VII, like Edward IV, was a strong king within whose council administrative competence, especially in legal and financial matters, and willingness to serve the crown were the avenues to advancement.[73] Similarly, while formal designation as a king's councillor gave a man a status which was both honorific and which associated him with the regime,[74] any person might be brought within the compass of conciliar work at a moment's notice by royal command. This tendency was most marked again in respect of legal expertise. The two chief justices, the chief baron of the exchequer and the three leading sergeants-at-law were invariably sworn councillors.[75] In addition selected lawyers – and others of ability – attended Henry VII's council, being admitted to the king's counsels by royal requirement. They sat as equals 'amongst the councillors' in star chamber and elsewhere, frequently or infrequently according to instructions, but were not as yet sworn.[76]

Henry VII's council was at work from the first months of his reign.[77] There was naturally much to be done in the way of appointments and arrests between September 1485 and January 1486. By the latter month, however, the balance between executive and judicial work had been fully restored, and the council worked within both areas at meetings during the Hilary term 1486.[78] Plenary sessions of the council in star chamber were held on 25 and 31 January; 6, 8, 10, 15-18, 24 February; and 4 March.[79] The litigation taken was primarily between private parties. Official, government action was nevertheless not absent, although it was inevitably inseparable from politics at this early date. Thus on 15 February Sir Edward Grey, Viscount Lisle, was dismissed of riot 'because the matter is taken to the kinges handes, as his atturney certified'.[80] After the council meeting of 4 March and the dissolution of parliament on that day, Henry embarked on his tour of the north, leaving selected councillors on duty in London over Easter.[81] Those to whom charge of the capital was entrusted numbered fourteen councillors and 'somme other', unfortunately unidentified, 'persons' who sat in star chamber on five days, namely 16-18 March and 4-5 April.[82] The king ended his tour on 5 June.[83] From 7 to 9 June he personally presided over the council in star chamber.[84] At these meetings, forty of the council were occupied with business which ranged from a decision to send for the mayor of London to explain security precautions in the capital, the appointment of a delegation to treat with the Scottish ambassadors and the obtaining of news from Calais, to the pronouncement of a decree in a complex maritime case and the issue of process and the entry of appearance in routine private litigation.[85] It was decided to reassemble the council 'on mondaie before noone', and on 12 June the lords indeed met and resolved to command the mayor of Bristol by privy seal to do justice to Ferdinando de Santiago, a Spaniard, 'or otherwyse to appere *coram Rege*'.[86] The next day Henry VII again presided in star chamber.[87] The session was attended by twenty-six councillors, and both executive and judicial business was taken. The remainder of June and July 1486 saw eighteen further council meetings of a similar nature;[88] and thereafter a fully active and numerously attended council settled down, holding regular formal meetings in star chamber during the law terms, at which it was frequently directed by the king in person.[89]

But it was not in star chamber that conciliar decisions were taken in the two most important areas of domestic government. The formulation of fiscal and enforcement policies was at first undertaken by Bray,[90] Lovell,[91] Morton[92] and Fox,[93] in liaison with the king and other ministers, and after the deaths of Morton and Bray was equally firmly vested in the members of the prerogative tribunals known as the council learned in the law and the conciliar court of audit.[94] The importance of the executive matters retained for discussion in star chamber should never be underplayed, and there were real debates at these meetings. The council in plenary session was, however, a consultative rather than a policy-making body under Henry VII. It formed a point of contact between the crown, its ministers and the politically active members of society, especially the lay nobility.[95] In this respect it was of vital importance to government, since the first Tudor king's demand for royal service which was both arduous and intellectually exacting had tended to exclude the peerage from active conciliar work. It is not insignificant that Henry VII's council was concerned in star chamber with precisely those secrets which had to be opened to all councillors. The council considered the issues which, of necessity, had to secure the support of the magnates while still in the policy stage, namely internal security, the armed defences and foreign affairs.[96]

The extent to which the early Tudor council was amorphous is now more fully appreciated. The executive and judicial work of the council in star chamber was only the principal manifestation of conciliar activity under Henry VII: 'All that was ever done by the council was done by groups of councillors, the composition of which varied greatly from time to time and according to the nature of the business.'[97] Councillors might be employed on the king's affairs at formal meetings at Westminster in star chamber, in attendance at court during a royal progress, within the royal household, in the council learned or the court of audit, or even still in chancery without in any way changing their status as members of the whole body. There were no 'committees' of the council. There was no delegation or relegation of business by the council, the only exception being when it was necessary to nominate representatives to treat with foreign ambassadors.[98] The protean forms of the king's council were nothing more than the king's councillors at work whenever and wherever they were needed. Despite this fluidity, however, certain manifestations of conciliar activity outside star chamber need to be identified. The council learned and the court of audit, while remaining elastic elements of the council, had each come to enjoy a limited degree of informal structure and separate development by the last years of the reign.[99] Similarly, while the council in star chamber and the council in attendance during a progress were theoretically the same institution, they did not comprise the same people when the king resolved to travel during the law terms, as in 1486 and 1494.[100] On these occasions it proved necessary to prescribe who should remain in London and who should join the tour.[101] The lord chancellor, being obliged to remain in the capital during term, was deputed to preside at meetings of the council in star chamber during royal absences.[102] Council meetings on progress would have been directed by the king. But even Henry VII could not supervise personally all aspects of conciliar work out of town, especially where justice was concerned, and a 'president of the council' managed the business created by suitors who appeared where the king was, bringing their petitions and bills of complaint for adjudication by the council.[103] The first president was Richard Fox, keeper of the privy seal,[104] and under him the king's councillors took an active part in the hearing of suits on progress.[105] In the later years of Henry VII, however, routine litigation was usually handled by a group of lesser councillors, some of whom probably never acted as councillors for any other purpose.[106] The dean of the chapel royal of the household, the king's almoner and the royal chaplains were consistently members of the group.[107] Churchmen had been traditionally employed in such capacities. Also included were the doctors of canon or civil law, and normally some common lawyers, the latter providing the expertise needed for the adjudication of the legal problems involved.[108] The evidence is scanty; but it seems that Henry VII's council in attendance resumed and developed a judicial function similar to that exercised under the Yorkists by an itinerant 'council of requests'.[109]

The species of conciliar activity under Henry VII most distinctive in the contemporary mind nevertheless remained 'the honorable Court of Counsaill' in the *camera stellata*. The council there constituted a sedentary forum for litigation during the law terms and was recognised as such by litigants and lawyers alike.[110] William Warham, Henry VII's last chancellor, recalled early in Wolsey's ascendancy how, about the year 1502, litigants had appeared in star chamber 'in the said Courte' before 'the said late kynges Councell, and in the whole Courte the said parties before the said Councell were indifferently herd'.[111] The court at this date was neither separately established nor institutionally differentiated from the council acting in other capacities: matters of justice were entertained by the council on a purely *ad hoc* basis when time permitted after the completion of executive discussions at council meetings.[112] The point was not reached in the reign of Henry VII at which timetabling of conciliar business and the preparation in advance of detailed agenda were required. When, however, Sir John Paston's correspondent could write from London in 1494 that the council had been so busy on the king's affairs that 'my Lord Chawnsler kept not the Ster Chawmber thys viij days', the suggestion is strong that the council was popularly regarded as having a court-like existence and that an interruption in its regular work was a matter for casual as well as professional comment.[113]

The jurisdiction exercised by the council in star chamber was both criminal and civil.[114] Limitations were negatively defined by a number of medieval statutes which declared *inter alia* that the council should not determine matters of freehold, or try cases touching life and limb.[115] The former limitation was difficult to respect in the late fifteenth and early sixteenth centuries, especially if the council was to maintain intact its traditional reputation for equitable proceedings. These were years rich in litigation about land: political and social change, accompanied by numerous doubtful claims and the traffic in pretended titles, ensured a ready supply of litigants in all the courts.[116] Prevailing conditions at common law rendered the council particularly vulnerable to the complaints and petitions of men who required relief from the potentially inequitable rigour of legal procedure, who sought an enforceable settlement by the arbitration of the king's councillors, or who were simply trying out their luck. The second limitation was generally adhered to. The council as a court avoided treason and felony. Although felons occasionally appeared in star chamber, they did so only if some technicality needed to be settled before a case at common law could begin,[117] or if maintenance or the malfeasance or corruption of local officials interrupted the due legal process.[118] When the anonymous author of the note prefatory to the Ellesmere extracts declared that the court of star chamber heard 'of murder and treason' in the reign of Henry VII, he was – like Mill, Lambarde and Hudson – confusing the council's work as a court with its role as an administrative body.[119] Admittedly the council was limited in respect of its punishments rather than in the matter tried. Felony was theoretically no bar if it was punished as a misdemeanour, as became clearer in the reign of Henry VIII.[120] Nevertheless, the work of Mr C. G. Bayne established that the litigation which came before Henry VII's council in star chamber was primarily civil, though disguised as criminal, and between private parties.[121] Even the council's traditional jurisdiction in riot was largely set in motion by private bills and only very rarely by the government.[122] Bayne's conclusions are broadly untarnished by the discovery that the arrangement of the misnamed *Star Chamber Proceedings, Henry VII* at the Public Record Office failed to include roughly one-third of the documents which survive for the reign, the remainder having come to light amongst unsorted miscellanea left by the arrangers.[123] Although Bayne's total of one hundred and ninety-four cases extant for the twenty-four years is thus invalidated, the real count being nearer three hundred,[124] the proportional distribution of the suits between civil and criminal subjects remains more or less constant. Similarly, of the suits not known to Bayne, almost all began with the filing of a bill of complaint or petition by a private party. There are, however, instances of proceedings before Henry VII's council in star chamber which were initiated by the government.[125]

Two-thirds of the cases heard by the council in star chamber under Henry VII were private suits in which offences against public order – riot, rout, unlawful assembly or assault – were alleged by the plaintiff.[126] But in three-quarters of these the supposed violent acts were entirely or partially fictitious.[127] The position was that lawyers had resolved to introduce their clients' English bills of complaint with verbatim translations of words of art borrowed from the common law. Where the writ of trespass set out that the defendant came *vi et armis* and *in AB insultum fecit,* model bills in star chamber alleged that the defendant came 'in riotous manner', 'with great power and might', or 'with force of arms offensive and defensive', and 'made assawte' upon the plaintiff or his agent.[128] The most frequent complaint was that defendants came riotously with force of arms and evicted the plaintiff from his house or land; and, as might be expected, an unquiet title invariably lay behind the case.[129] In addition about half the purely civil (i.e. non-disguised) suits in star chamber were also about land or its management.[130] These comprised questions of title and possession, tortious enclosure, copyhold tenure, nonpayment of rent and illegal distraint. The subjects of the remaining civil suits which were heard before Henry VII's council range from disputes over municipal franchises and trade and commerce to wardship and villeinage.[131]

There need be no doubt that the council, having received petitions concerned with what emerged as purely civil business, actually adjudicated on them when it found no criminal offence disclosed. Warham observed how under Henry VII bills of this type were 'by the said late kynges pleasure . . . sent in to the Ster Chamber there to be ordred and determynyd'.[132] Decrees for the possession of land are known to have been pronounced by the council in star chamber for the abbot of Conway, Sir Ralph Ashton, Elizabeth Ashfelde and Isabel Mortimer in 1486; Mary Hopwarde in 1487; John Woodhall, the abbot of St Mary without York and William Doget in 1492; and Robert Inkarsall and John Steward in 1493.[133] Doget's case turned out to be of additional interest as it established the extent to which the king and council regarded their jurisdiction in star chamber as the pinnacle of the English judicial system. The suit also demonstrated the primitive axiom that kings had a duty to render justice out of their own mouths and through those of their intimate councillors. Doget and his wife Jane claimed the manor of Curson's in Norfolk against Sir John Radcliffe, who

allegedly held it by 'mayntenance and Riottes'.[134] The
defendant appeared but failed to file his answer by the day appointed. He was therefore recalled before the council to make
answer under penalty of £100.[135] At the hearing, the king
himself played a leading part in the debate, deciding each of
the several points at issue.[136] Judgment was given for the
plaintiffs and the decree was entered in the council register.[137]
Within a year, however, the case had been resumed by the
defendant in the court of common pleas.[138] Henry VII was
informed of this and, personally presiding in star chamber on
16 February 1493 and 'speaking with great force before all the
council', commanded a privy seal to be issued to the judges,
ordering them to respite their proceedings until further
notice.[139] The king was greatly displeased by the unsuccessful
defendant's initiation of parallel litigation at common law.
That the council promptly overruled pleas to the effect that
matters of freehold were *ultra vires* its jurisdiction is confirmed
by the exclusion of counsel in 1506 from future appearance in
star chamber 'for his disobedience' in advising a client 'to
make none answere to the title of Lande' depending before the
council.[140]

No more than a tenth of the litigation before Henry VII's
council in star chamber was criminal in content.[141] This is
perhaps less surprising than might at first be thought. The
council was barred from capital punishments, which could
only be imposed at common law or by act of attainder, and the
precise nature of 'misdemeanour' as an area between felony
and civil pleadings was a matter still surrounded by obscurity
in the late fifteenth century.[142] It is certain that the early
Tudor council enjoyed with full statutory sanction a comprehensive jurisdiction in riot and cognate offences,[143] and
that the lords of the council were traditionally regarded as a
source of equitable remedy in the face of acts contrary to
public justice, especially corrupt verdicts by juries and inquests, maintenance and embracery, subornation and perjury,
the abuse of legal machinery and the malfeasance of officers. It
is also very likely that Henry VII wished to develop the council's jurisdiction in misdemeanour, not merely to provide relief

for the complainant but also to punish the actors of such transgressions by fine or imprisonment. Only rarely, however, did the council in star chamber receive bills or petitions in which misdemeanours were alleged as the sole matter of the complaint. The king's subjects generally brought crime to light only when they had in view an interest of their own; and such interests, notably damages, ensured that the private denunciation of crime was most often cloaked in the garb of civil pleadings in trespass at common law. In about thirty instances, matters essentially criminal were related by private parties in star chamber and were considered actionable by Henry VII's council. Half of these were cases of riot, following events which had constituted or were likely to provoke serious disturbances of the peace, all amounting to much more than the usual show of force which accompanied disputes about land or the chance cudgelling that was common in an age when careless talk was followed by physical rather than verbal riposte.[144] Other 'misdemeanours' pleaded in star chamber included the purchase of a title 'hangyng in pley and variaunce' and its maintenance,[145] two cases of embracery,[146] four complaints of the malfeasance of sheriffs,[147] embezzlement,[148] defamation,[149] forgery,[150] fraud,[151] the razure and falsification of a record in the court of common pleas,[152] false imprisonment[153] and felony in circumstances of flagrant maintenance.[154]

In addition to these private suits, a handful of official criminal prosecutions were initiated before the council in star chamber under Henry VII. Three such cases, probably four, are extant, all but one of which were primarily for riot.[155] The exception was for a corrupt verdict by a jury.[156] In official prosecutions the attorney-general moved for the king, filing a written information or a bill of 'articles' to which the defendants were obliged to provide written answers or (presumably) a sworn confession. They were then examined on oath upon each detail of their answers and on any matters arising, the examinations being conducted *viva voce* and the statements being taken down more or less verbatim by the clerk of the council.[157] Perjury by defendants in their answers or depositions was severely punished if detected. [158] That official prosecutions in star chamber were the exception rather than the rule is, however, clearly suggested by the case begun in 1488 against Thomas lord Dacre, Henry lord Clifford, the abbot of Holm Cultram, the mayor of Carlisle, Sir Christopher Moresby, Launcelot Thrilkeld and Thomas Curwen. [159] The articles against the defendants alleged 'insurreccions and ryattes' committed in clashes shortly after Easter 1488 between the rival private armies retained in the west marches by Dacre and Moresby. The defendants variously appeared before the king and council in star chamber on 28 November and 1 December 1488, and on 5 February 1489. Henry VII was furious with them. Dacre, Clifford and Moresby were imprisoned in the Fleet and the first two fined £20 apiece. [160] So minimal a fine was more than compensated for by the king's wrath. Henry conducted the examination of the defendants personally, and took a memorandum of a deposition in his own hand on the dorse of the bill of articles. [161] The memorandum reveals the exceptional nature of the case. In the course of their rioting 'with Trompettes blowyng in fourme of warre', the defendants had succeeded in creating a diplomatic incident with the Scots. One 'Parkes the Scottisseman' had been 'arrested' during the fighting, and the king had regarded the matter as potentially fatal to 'peax betwixt the Realmes'. [162] The subsequent investigations were therefore thorough, examining all 'reteyndors', riots, extortions, oppressions, maintenance and 'bering' in the county of Cumberland. Proceedings were taken throughout in star chamber, no doubt as an example to others.

Generally, however, little was done under Henry VII in the way of official prosecution of crime before the council in star chamber. The council in plenary session was not a body sufficiently homogeneous for the certain management of government suits. A smaller group of councillors was required which had a fixed composition and continuity of membership, and an assured presence of legal experts. Henry VII therefore revived the system by which the law-enforcement function of the council was concentrated into 'special' tribunals. [163] The most

important of these was the court established in 1487 by the so-
called act '*pro camera stellata*'.[164] The court was to suppress riot
and offences contrary to public justice 'uppon bill or informa-
cion ... for the kyng or any other'.[165] The statute pulled
together existing legislation by identifying as cognate offences
maintenance, livery, indentures, retaining, embracery, the im-
panelling of corrupt juries, the false returning of verdicts
through bribery, and riot and unlawful assembly for overawing
courts.[166] The tribunal was composed of the lord chancellor,
lord treasurer and keeper of the privy seal, or two of them,
'calling' also a bishop, a temporal lord of the council and the
two chief justices. An opinion of 1493 held that the three
office-holders were the judges of the court; the other four were
assessors only, but they had to be summoned and consulted.[167]
The extant proceedings of the court entirely confirm its status
as a ministerial tribunal distinct from the council in star
chamber or elsewhere. The only coincidence between the
tribunal and star chamber was that it sometimes met in the
camera stellata,[168] though it sat more frequently in the
chancellor's own court.[169]

The statute of 1487 represented the climax of the Lancastrian trend towards ministerial government in areas concerned with the 'polacye and good rule of this realme'.[170] It did
nothing for the council of Henry VII as an institution other
than to complement its work by the better identification and
punishment of misdemeanour. The act had, of course, omitted
one major method for the perversion of justice and administration, namely perjury by the parties to litigation themselves and
by the panels of juries and inquests, especially inquests of
office.[171] A statute therefore passed through parliament in
1495, almost certainly as the result of discussion on the point
at a council meeting in November 1494,[172] which enacted that
complaints of perjury handed to the justices who tried the
cases in which the offence was alleged to have occurred were to
be sent to the chancellor and heard by himself, the treasurer,
the chief justices and the master of the rolls.[173] Such
proceedings as survive for this second court indicate that it
operated in a manner similar to that of 1487.[174] With the death

of Henry VII, however, both tribunals fell into abeyance despite their statutory authority, casualties – like the council learned – of the reaction against 'special' courts in government.

2

Wolsey's Management of the Council

POLICY AND THE COUNCIL

From the death of Henry VII to the time of Wolsey's appointment as chief minister of Henry VIII, the work of the king's council continued without interruption, although the council shrank marginally in size. The story is most likely true that the lady Margaret Beaufort selected an 'inner ring' of councillors to advise her young and inexperienced grandson and to manage the affairs of state.[1] The records confirm the existence and activity of an inner ring, the 'most trusted' councillors of Henry VII, consisting of Thomas Howard, then earl of Surrey, Richard Fox, bishop of Winchester, Thomas Ruthal, bishop of Durham, Charles Somerset, the lord Herbert, George Talbot, earl of Shrewsbury, Sir Henry Marney, Sir Thomas Englefield, Sir Thomas Lovell, William Warham, archbishop of Canterbury and lord chancellor, and others;[2] but attendances at the plenary sessions of the council in the *camera stellata* during term-time were in no way restricted to this group and appear to have been much the same as under Henry VII. Lord Herbert of Cherbury was in error when he failed to discover the judges at work in the new king's council.[3] The presence in star chamber ranged from eight (frequent) to about twenty-five (rare), comprising those of the inner ring who were in London, to whom were added the traditional composition of temporal lords, ecclesiastics, household knights, and the judges and other common lawyers.[4] Duly assembled in star chamber, the council was as imposing as ever. Henry VIII, however, rarely attended formal council meetings. Warham, as lord chancellor, therefore presided in star chamber;[5] the king's interests were represented by the members of the inner ring, who travelled frequently between the itinerant royal court and London. This may not have marked too great a change from the later years of Henry VII; the first Tudor seems not to have regularly attended the council in star chamber after 1504.[6]

The situation in the first months of the new reign was markedly changed only by the popular anti-monarchical reaction released by the death of Henry VII, the fall of Empson and Dudley, and the consequent collapse of Henry VII's comprehensive network of enforcement by recognisance before the king in his chamber. Early in July 1509 the council approved the issue of general commissions of *oyer et terminer*. These were the commissions under which Empson and Dudley were indicted, tried and condemned; but they constituted a nationwide inquiry to redress grievances.[7] The commissioners were empowered to inquire through juries concerning treasons, murders, rapes, insurrections, rebellions, felonies, trespasses, conspiracies, forestallings, regratings, maintenance, embraceries, riots, routs, unlawful assemblies, illegal retaining and other offences. Presentments were determined by due legal process.[8] However, while the council's intention may have been to appease resentment against Henry VII's prerogative government by the provision of a regular, accepted, common-law facility, such laudable motives were clearly not appreciated. On 11 October following, the council after lengthy debate accepted the view that 'by the demeanor of the people the contynuaunce of the said Oyer Determyner sholde be to them bothe chargeable and painfull'; and since the judges reported that 'in asmuche as the substance of all the great, weightye and urgent matters and busynes' was concluded, it was recommended that the commissions should be ended.[9] When the matter was reconsidered on 14 November, the council added the argument that few of the cases taken by the commissioners had actually concerned the criminal offences 'for which suche Comissions sholde be graunted'; civil and 'meane' pleas should be determined by writ before the ordinary courts at Westminster.[10] The commissions were finally revoked by proclamation twelve days later, the explanation given being based on the inconvenience and expense incurred by parties and juries.[11] This ignored the difficulty of deciding cases at the centre which required local evidence, but confirms that the reason for ending the commissions lay in the annoyance they were causing.

At the same meetings, the council was also exercised by the reaction against 'by-courts', especially those concerned with financial administration and accounting – the council learned and the conciliar court of audit. It was thought to be 'expedient and necessarye to Adnulle the said Courtes that they be noe more used'.[12] This opinion secured the approval of the council, though not because the prerogative courts of Henry VII's later years were considered to be oppressive to the subject, but because 'the kinges Righte and tytell in proces of tyme sholde perishe for lacke of matter of Recorde . . . for the kinges highnes cannot be intituled by Recorde but by matter of Recorde in Courte of Aucthority'.[13] The other argument used, that subjects could not be lawfully discharged for payments made in those courts, reflected the exchequer's attitude which led to the series of statutes establishing the general surveyors.[14]

Mutterings in corners and complaints about prerogative courts, though indisputably serious, were nevertheless insufficient to interfere with the regular work of the council in its executive and judicial spheres. The council in star chamber under Warham's presidency debated all matters of state and the formulation and execution of policy;[15] and, sitting as a court, the council heard cases of riot, forcible entry, unquiet title, rescue, alleged felony unpunished at common law, perjury, contempt of judicial process, tortious enclosure, fraud, and municipal and trade disputes.[16] As in the reign of Henry VII, this litigation was almost invariably at the suit of private parties; however, two official prosecutions are known to have been initiated for serious rioting.[17] Whether a decline in the quantity of judicial work in star chamber was a consequence of the reaction against conciliar courts in and after 1509 is perhaps less certain than was at first thought.[18] The sources are defective, and a change in the clerkship of the council shortly after the death of Henry VII may have resulted in less efficient record-keeping for a time.[19] What is not uncertain is that Wolsey revived and developed the judicial function of the council. The cardinal's policy was first to restore and to reabsorb into the council in star chamber much of the conciliar jurisdiction which had been exercised during the previous reign. Secondly, Wolsey imposed on the council courts his conviction that the availability of conciliar justice in suits between party and party was a great public benefit. The minister's efforts and their consequences did much to dictate the development of the Tudor and Stuart conciliar courts, despite the need for further reorganisation and establishment later in the reign of Henry VIII.

The council during Wolsey's supremacy was as large as it had been in the reign of Henry VII. Some one hundred and twenty persons have been identified as having attended the council in star chamber during the cardinal's chancellorship, this figure including both those who were full councillors and those admitted to the king's counsels by royal or ministerial favour.[20] The slight depletion of the ranks at formal meetings which had occurred between 1509 and 1515 was partly alleviated by the admission of new councillors,[21] but was mainly eliminated by the more regular attendance of existing ones. The latter circumstance was itself consequential upon the eclipse of the potentially exclusive inner ring and the rejuvenation by the cardinal of star chamber. The eclipse of any form of cabinet within the council was inevitable under a minister of Wolsey's inclinations; rejuvenation was ensured by the cardinal's policy and personal drive. Attendances at council meetings in star chamber after Wolsey's appointment as lord chancellor (on 24 December 1515) sometimes exceeded thirty persons. On 2 May 1516, a presence of thirty-five headed by Henry VIII in person, Wolsey, the bishops of Lincoln and Ely, the dukes of Norfolk, Buckingham and Suffolk, and the earls of Surrey and Worcester, heard the cardinal address 'a notable and Elegant Oration' to the king.[22] Such events at which the king was present, however, were exceptional, being great assemblies of the council rather than meetings. At that of 2 May 1516, Wolsey's speech was followed by the appearance of the earl of Northumberland before the presence.[23] The earl made his submission to the king and was committed to the Fleet prison for contempt of the council's jurisdiction in private suits.[24] Wolsey then pronounced his final judgment in the case of the gilds of Newcastle-upon-Tyne,[25] after which the councillors repaired to a special dinner at Lambeth, also attended by Henry VIII, his queen and his younger sister, the dowager queen of France.[26] The largest attendance at a council meeting in this period was on 27 October 1519 when fifty-four persons were present (again including the king).[27] Such rare occasions apart, however, attendances were smaller and the average presence varied from between eleven (frequent) to twenty-five (less usual) of the council.[28]

Although the Henrician council registers are missing, the loss of record material is far from being so great as historians have supposed.[29] It is possible to reconstruct a fair proportion of the missing documentation from closely related sources: notably the Ellesmere extracts, the *Star Chamber Proceedings,* the chancery rolls and files, the *State Papers,* and exchequer records. Evidence, in varying detail, of five hundred and thirty-six council meetings in star chamber can be discovered for the period of Wolsey's chancellorship.[30] The lists of the presence are extant for sixty-three of these meetings and indicate that thirty-one councillors in addition to Wolsey attended the council with the greatest frequency.[31] The activity on conciliar work of these same persons is also amply evident from the *Proceedings* and from the *Letters and Papers of Henry VIII.*

Clerics

Thomas Wolsey, lord chancellor and archbishop of York

Thomas Ruthal, keeper of the privy seal and bishop of Durham (died 1523)

Cuthbert Tunstall, master of the rolls (1516-22), bishop of London (from 1522) and keeper of the privy seal (from 1523)

John Islip, abbot of Westminster

Charles Booth, bishop of Hereford

Temporal Lords

Thomas Howard, duke of Norfolk and treasurer (died 1524)

Charles Brandon, duke of Suffolk

Thomas Howard, earl of Surrey (to 1524), treasurer (from 1522) and duke of Norfolk (from 1524)

Thomas Grey, marquis of Dorset

George Talbot, earl of Shrewsbury and steward of the household

George Neville, lord Burgavenny

Thomas Boleyn knight, created viscount Rochford (1525)

Thomas Docwra, prior of St John (died 1527)

Knights

Edward Belknap

John Cutt, under-treasurer (to 1521)

Robert Drury

William Fitzwilliam, treasurer of the household (from 1524)

Thomas Lovell, treasurer of the household (died 1524)

Henry Marney, chancellor of the duchy, keeper of the privy seal (14 February 1523; died 24 May following)

Thomas More, under-treasurer (1521–5),
   chancellor of the duchy (1525–9)

Thomas Neville

Richard Weston

Andrew Windsor, keeper of the great wardrobe

Richard Wingfield, chancellor of the duchy (1523-5)

Henry Wyatt

Justices

Richard Broke
Robert Brudenell, C.J.C.P. (from 1520)
Humphrey Coningsby
Richard Elyot
John Erneley, C.J.C.P. (to 1520)
John Fineux, C.J.K.B.
Lewis Pollard

Since Henry VIII rarely attended formal council meetings, he relied on Wolsey to manage his council and keep him abreast of affairs either in person or by correspondence. At judicial sessions in star chamber, the chancellor directed proceedings and pronounced such orders and decrees as were appropriate in the name of king and council. Early signs of the prominence of the council's judicial work under Wolsey were to be further emphasised by the reduction in the discussion of the affairs of state at council meetings, itself the consequence of the cardinal's supremacy. Although the minister could not refuse the advice of the Howards and Brandons, Marneys and Lovells, who attended both the council and the royal court, he could reduce consultation to the barest minimum, and the cardinal was abrupt even with leading councillors.[32] Discussion of affairs of state was almost entirely confined to domestic issues. No longer did the council hold regular debates on foreign affairs and defence, as in the reign of Henry VII. Despite the scale and expense of England's renewed continental involvement, policy decisions in these areas were despatched by Wolsey himself in liaison with the king, with the occasional intervention of whichever councillors had happened to secure Henry's ear while accompanying the royal progress. Yet, far from the council's suffering decline or decay as a body during the fourteen years of Wolsey's power, the membership and frequency of meetings were fully maintained. For example, in 1516 the council in star chamber met not less than 14 times in Hilary term, 18 times in Easter term, 33 in Trinity and 31 in Michaelmas terms. In 1524 there were not less than 20 meetings in Hilary term, 22 in Easter, and 37 in both Trinity and Michaelmas terms.[33]

It should not be thought that the council ceased to be a real governing institution during Wolsey's political ascendancy. The council supervised the swearing-in of sheriffs and justices of the peace, made arrangements for the provision of food in times of scarcity, fixed and enforced the prices of many commodities, especially cloth, debated projected legislation, and acted to restrain the extent of vagrancy in the capital.[34] There were debates which were far from being mere formality: many must have been as real as that of 25 April 1516 regarding the latest episode in the current bitter hostility between London and alien merchants and craftsmen which culminated in the Evil May Day riots of 1517.[35] Elaborate investigations were decided on to identify the handwriting of the authors of two 'slanderous' bills, which had been nailed to the doors of St Paul's and the church of All Hallows Barking in Tower Street.[36] The volume of the council's executive contribution to government was nevertheless insufficient to maintain the regularity of its meetings. It was the expansion of the council's judicial activity after 1515, a reality firmly established by the extant records of the council and the council courts, which provided more than sufficient business to enable the council to flourish as an institution in an otherwise doubtful period of its history.

The large-scale resumption of the council's judicial operations under Wolsey became apparent within the first four years of his office. First, a policy to impose 'indifferent justice' upon the king's realm was announced in the 'Oration' delivered at the great assembly of the council on 2 May 1516.[37]

> The moste reverent father had this daye to the kinges heighnes a notable and Elegant Oration in Englishe wherin he made open to his most excellent providence the enormityes usuallye exercised in this his Realme to the derogacion of indifferent Justice as well as the Causes of the Continuaunce of the same enormityes. For the redresse and reformacion wherof the same moste reverent father advertised his heighnes in the name of the hole Counsellors of certayne provisions by theire diligent studye excogitate.

Henry VIII delivered an acknowledgement of Wolsey's speech, which expressed his steadfast desire to maintain his coronation oath and required 'his most honorable Councellors, as his Judges and ministers of his Lawes . . . to followe and execute the same [provisions]'. [38] The subsequent humiliation of the earl of Northumberland was clearly intended as exemplary; even in his judgment for the gild merchants of Newcastle, the last item of the day's agenda, the minister was at pains to emphasise that the matters in dispute had led to violence and the abuse of judicial process. [39] Wolsey's policy generally aimed at the enforcement of the law in the existing courts of common law, with an overall supervisory role firmly assigned to the council. As such, it was soon put into effect. On 3 May 1516, Henry VIII's elder sister, Queen Margaret of Scotland, entered London and lodged at Baynard's Castle. [40] When she subsequently met the king's council, George lord Hastings and Sir Richard Sacheverell were accompanied by retainers in livery. [41] Wolsey began an immediate investigation into the prevalence of illegal retaining and related offences amongst members of the council, requiring full details of circumstances and events. Sir Edward Guildford was compelled to inform against George Neville, lord Burgavenny. [42] Lord Hastings and Sacheverell were examined in star chamber; Thomas Grey, marquis of Dorset, was then accused; and all three were bound to their future appearance and to good behaviour. [43] At first it appeared that the offenders would be formally prosecuted and punished in star chamber, [44] but this was not Wolsey's intention. Serious breaches of the law required a more effective deterrent than a humiliation before the council, followed by a brief sojourn in the Fleet. Informations were therefore filed in king's bench: these variously charged Sacheverell, lord Hastings, lord Burgavenny and the marquis of Dorset with retaining in breach of the statutes, riot, rout, unlawful assembly and trespass. [45]

Wolsey re-emphasised his policy of enforcement before the king at three further assemblies of the council on 14 May 1517, and 27 and 28 October 1519. On 14 May 1517 the government reaction to Evil May Day and its aftermath was embodied in the *acta* of the council. [46] The official line, announced first to the council in star chamber and then to the mayor and aldermen of the city, assembled in Westminster hall with the four hundred or so prisoners taken in London during the disturbances, was one of clemency with an end to the earlier series of executions for treason. [47] Wolsey, in addition, offered advice to Henry VIII concerning 'the enormyties and thinges misbehaved and misordered within this Relme'. [48] On 27 October 1519 Wolsey delivered another 'notable Oration' concerning the 'due administration' of justice. [49] The following day's timetable was arranged once more for its theatrical and exemplary effect: the day saw the submission of Sir William Bulmer for wearing the duke of Buckingham's livery in the royal presence, followed by the final hearing of the case against Sir Matthew Browne and Sir John A Legh, two of three Surrey justices accused of 'grete mayntenance, embrasery and beryng'. [50]

The cardinal's plan was, however, not confined to the investigation and prosecution of existing offenders. It extended to administrative measures. In November 1519, Thomas Ruthal was to be found supervising the drafting of new articles of instruction to be read on behalf of Wolsey and the council at the annual swearing-in of sheriffs and justices of the peace. [51] The document, which declared the king's zeal 'for the trew and indifferent ministracion of hys lawys and Justice', [52] clearly harked back to the minister's speeches of 2 May 1516 and 27 October 1519. These had likewise desired 'thindifferent ministracion of Justice to all persounes aswell heighe as lowe'. [53] The articles explained how sheriffs were to 'truly and indifferently execute the kynges processes, wretes [sic], warauntes and comaundementes', and instructed them in the due exercising of their office. In particular, sheriffs were to do all in their power to prevent their own officers from 'embezzling' the king's writs and precepts, and making 'untrue retorne uppon them'. Panels for inquests and juries were to be composed of such persons 'as be most suffycient and most nere to the place where the mater or cause is alleged', and who were most 'indifferent'. Similarly, sheriffs were not to 'take eny money or other thyng or promise' for making a corrupt panel, nor were they to accept jurors at the nomination of their undersheriffs or bailiffs, 'but such as they will swere and afferme by there halydome othe' to be impartial. [54] After the initial reading of the new instructions (on 21 November 1519), they were ordered to be printed. [55] Wolsey's resolution to attack the corruption of sheriffs resulted also in an examination of the oath on which they were sworn. Subsequent modifications to the text of the oath were slight, but the provision was inserted that the sheriff should empanel only those persons 'most next, most sufficient and not suspecte nor procured'. [56] The revised oath was to be printed alongside the new instructions. [57] The cardinal was severe with those sheriffs who practised the abuses and 'craftie Invencions' he so deplored. Sir John Savage, whose family had held the office of sheriff of Worcestershire in fee since 1497, had been committed to the Tower by Wolsey in June 1516 and was comprehensively indicted in king's bench during the following Michaelmas term for his numerous acts of malfeasance. [58] He was later deprived in favour of Sir William Compton. [59] The minister's other measures included several attempts to restrict the 'mischief' resulting from the abuse of sanctuary, the problems arising from the availability of the privilege at the Priory of St John and Westminster Abbey being debated in star chamber before Henry VIII on 10 and 11 November 1519. [60] Also in star chamber on 14 October 1518, the judges and sergeants-at-law had been commanded to file reports to the council concerning offences against justice in the country: 'that is to say, whoe be Retaynors or oppressors, or maintaynors of wrongfull Causes, or otherwise misbehaved persons'. [61] By the following term, additional inquiries had been extended to the localities themselves. [62] Those officers who were suspected of having been negligent in the work of enforcement were summoned to appear before the council, and enjoined not to depart 'untyll suche tyme as they have made theire purgacion whye they have not donne their dewtyes'. [63]

Wolsey's policy restored to the council, concentrated in star chamber, the enforcement jurisdiction which it had exercised in the previous reign. It also of itself generated many bills of complaint addressed to the council in star chamber. These bills alleged crimes unpunished at law, inadequate and negligent law enforcement, perjury and the abuse of legal machinery, and the malfeasance of officers.[64] The activity at the council board during the first four years of Wolsey's supremacy had done much to encourage the popular impression that the cardinal's enthusiasm for justice caused him to put down the mighty while exalting the humbler folk.[65] In reality such cases as those of the earl of Northumberland,[66] Sir Robert Sheffield,[67] Sir Wiliam Bulmer and the Surrey justices,[68] and the prior of Norwich[69] were unworthy of public enthusiasm. As Pollard observed, Wolsey 'sometimes protests too much'.[70] The chancellor gloried in his presidency of the council, drew suits unto himself – especially those involving his conciliar colleagues – and pompously demonstrated his political power and personal intelligence in star chamber.[71] There was also much arrogance in the man. Pollard noted 'the heavy discount which has always to be made from Wolsey's appreciation of his own services'.[72] Writing to the king sixteen months after the first announcement of the policy of enforcement, Wolsey declared: 'And for yowr realme our lorde be thankyd yt was nevyr in such paxe nor tranquilyte. For all thys Summer I have had nowther of Ryat, felony nor forsebyll entre, but yt yowr lawys be in every plas indifferently mynystryd without leanying of any manner.'[73] There had, however, been an affray between the servants of Thomas Pygot, sergeant-at-law, and Sir Andrew Windsor, the councillor and keeper of the great wardrobe. To this Wolsey declared that he doubted not good example should come from their punishment and 'I trust at the next terme to lerne them lawe of the Stere chambre that they shalbi war howe from these forth they shall redres ther mater with ther handes'.[74] Six months later, the cardinal wrote to the bishop of Worcester at Rome that the kingdom was never in greater harmony and repose: *tanti enim justitiam et aequitatem facio, absit jactantiae crimen.*[75] By 1520 the enforcement policy was established as an axiom of the minister's government, and when Nicholas West, bishop of Ely, at the end of that year applauded the chancellor's honourable renown in the administration of 'indifferent justice' and the keeping of the realm in such tranquillity and peace as was never seen in England, we know that he indulged the gentle art of flattery.[76]

Popular acclaim for Wolsey's justice as favourable as that reported by Sebastian Giustinian in 1519 was, however, fortified by the second of the minister's measures.[77] This was the early encouragement of private litigation in the council courts. Wolsey, unlike most judges, was not shy to bring water to the mill. Fully aware of the difficulties of the contemporary common law while confident of his ability to supply the impartial justice he so desired as lord chancellor and keeper of the king's conscience, Wolsey boasted the renewed availability of the council courts, at the same time allowing in star chamber the relaxation of the procedural rules designed to facilitate the early elimination of frivolous suits.[78] The result was, as Edward Hall observed and the records now confirm, that the people complained without number and brought many an honest man to trouble and vexation.[79] There can be no doubt as to what happened: Wolsey's initial receptiveness to private litigation soon swamped the council courts with a deluge of work on real property.[80] As in the reign of Henry VII, a frequent cause of private litigation in the royal courts was the unquiet or pretended title to land, and the early sixteenth-century system ensured that men were only too ready to try their luck in any court which appeared favourable to their interest. The cardinal's motives in offering the facilities of conciliar jurisdiction, based as it was on the principles of equitable procedure, were laudable; in the face of the litigation which actually arrived, and the reluctance of individual litigants to settle their differences in a spirit of equitable compromise,[81] Wolsey quickly became bored and disillusioned, and the institutional history of the council courts under his rule became the story of how the chancellor organised his time and set about unloading the greater part of the burden he had created upon the shoulders of his conciliar colleagues.

STAR CHAMBER

Wolsey obliged the council to expand its reception of litigation in accordance with his desire to satisfy public demand for justice. That this obligation should apply to the judicial activity of the council both inside and outside the *camera stellata* was the clear consequence of the reality of the undivided king's council. Inside star chamber, the development of judicial business and procedure was the direct result of Wolsey's designs as worked out in the council court over which he personally presided. Outside it, development combined the immediate effects of the events in star chamber itself with an increasing element of self-determination. 'The Curte of the Sterre Chambre'[82] was nevertheless the major manifestation of early Tudor conciliar justice and was the council assembled in the *camera stellata* in plenary session to do justice to the subject. Justice and administration were frequently intermingled at council meetings in this period and litigants were entertained at the bar before the board (newly erected for the purpose), after the completion of the day's executive agenda. The composition of the court was therefore that of the executive council and the presence was generally between eleven and twenty-five persons, the standard attendance at routine meetings of the council. For obvious reasons, suitors were not received at the great assemblies of the council arranged by Wolsey when the king himself presided. Nor for that matter was executive discussion permitted then. However, with the development of timetabling and the attempted organisation of council business which was to come during Wolsey's supremacy, certain councillors became particularly associated with star chamber as a court.[83] These were first the principal office-holders who attended all council meetings irrespective of the business to be taken: the lord chancellor, the lord treasurer and the keeper of the privy seal. Secondly, those councillors were present who were professionally qualified to act as judges; and those persons who were particularly associated with conciliar justice in its protean forms attended when they were resident in London.

In the former group were the two chief justices, the chief baron of the exchequer, the puisne justices, the king's sergeants-at-law, the attorney-general, the solicitor-general, and the master of the rolls (a semi-professional). Associated with conciliar justice was the dean of the chapel royal of the household, the king's almoner, the dean of St Paul's, the abbot of Westminster, Dr John Longland while bishop of Lincoln, Thomas Docwra, prior of St John, John Bourchier, lord Berners, Sir Thomas Neville, Sir John Daunce, Sir Andrew Windsor, Sir John Husye, Sir Weston Browne, Sir Henry Wyatt, Sir Robert Drury, Sir Thomas More and William Ellis. The attendance of the remaining temporal lords, bishops and household officers was highly erratic and did not relate to the business actually before the council, though by sheer force of numbers these groups were naturally represented at most sessions in star chamber.

As in the reign of Henry VII, the matters dealt with by the council in star chamber under Wolsey covered all aspects of conciliar procedure: the issue of process and commissions; the filing of written pleadings by the parties; the examination of defendants and witnesses and the publication of their depositions; the taking of affidavits; the entry of appearances, admissions to attorney and recognisances; and the pronouncement of interlocutory orders, injunctions and final decrees. [84] In the early years of Wolsey's rule, much procedural work was still discharged in open court. The cardinal therefore soon became persuaded of the need for the better organisation of his own and the council's time. It was entered in the council *acta* for 17 June 1517 that: 'The Lordes have appointed to sitt here on the Mondaie, Tewesdaye, Thursedaye, and Satersdaie; and in the Chauncery on Wensdaye and Fridaie everye weeke, except there be ony daies of Retorne, and then sett partlye here, partlye in the Chauncerie.' [85] This order was followed on 13 October by a resolution that 'for reformacion of misorders and other enormityes in the kinges severall Courtes, the Lords have appointed to assemble here everye weeke twoe dayes, that is to saye Wensdaye and Fridaie'. [86] This latter order implied a recognition of the need for differentiation between the administrative and judicial work of the council in star chamber: better timetabling of the conciliar agenda was clearly preferable to the council's previous arrangement. Evidently, by Michaelmas term 1517, it was necessary to reserve two sitting days a week for hearing suits, both alleged 'enormities' and more traditional complaints, in order that the council might keep pace with the current rate of litigation.

In addition to better organisation and timetabling, Wolsey in and after 1517 invoked an ancient conciliar expedient by which work was diverted to committees. Three orders of 1517, 1518 and 1520 established a series of tribunals, staffed by standing 'commissioners' but hived off from star chamber, for the hearing and expedition of poor men's causes.[87] These courts were intended to be institutionally distinct from star chamber and did not sit in the *camera stellata* but elsewhere in the palace of Westminster (mainly in the white hall and the treasurer's chamber). The tribunals will be discussed therefore in conjunction with the justice of the council outside star chamber. In and after 1520, however, Wolsey referred the growing backlog of judicial business in star chamber to *ad hoc* committees of councillors, whose decisions were given in the name of the king's council in the star chamber and which were recorded as the *acta* of the council.[88] Most active in this capacity in 1521 and 1522 were Thomas Docwra, prior of St John, Sir Robert Drury, Sir John Husye, Sir Henry Wyatt, Sir John Daunce, Sir Weston Browne, Sir Thomas More and William Ellis.[89] Also employed on conciliar committees after 1522 were John Islip, abbot of Westminster, Sir Thomas Neville, Sir William Fitzwilliam, Sir Andrew Windsor, Sir Edward Belknap and Sir Henry Guildford.[90] The committees established by Wolsey in star chamber issued orders for process and commissions, entered the appearances of litigants and admitted them to attorney, took affidavits, and examined defendants and witnesses.[91] Committees sometimes also took cases on to publication and final hearing. Thus on 4 May 1521, after a committee had heard the arguments of counsel, 'the defendantes were imprisoned in the fleete and ordered to pay twenty nobles recompense to the playntif'.[92] On the following

3 July, Thomas Docwra, John Husye, Weston Browne and William Ellis sat in star chamber and a cause was decreede by them . . . between the prior of Sowthwike and Jone Holdepe for title of land. [It was] decreede for the prior'.[93] On 10 February 1522, Thomas Docwra, Robert Drury, Thomas More and William Ellis heard 'a cause of misdemenor . . . for carieng away the prioresse of Michell Kynton and taking away the goodes of that priory. And this cause being heard and debated, it was dismissed'.[94] The following 8 May, a witness was examined before Cuthbert Tunstall, Thomas Docwra, William Fitzwilliam, Thomas Neville and Andrew Windsor.[95] On 27 June 1523, Neville and Windsor ordered 'publication and reading of sundry deposicions of witnesses' and, after hearing counsel, decided for the plaintiffs.[96]

Individual councillors also sat alone in star chamber in order to discharge routine business on an 'out-of-court' basis. On 28 October 1523, John Islip sitting alone took an affidavit concerning the valid service of writs of *subpoena* and subsequently ordered the issue of writs of attachment against the defaulting parties.[97] In 1527 a witness was examined before Sir Thomas Neville sitting alone.[98] Most work despatched in this way was undertaken by William Ellis, a junior baron of the exchequer, who sat as a one-man committee for most of the 1520s.[99] Ellis specialised in referring cases 'to the hearing of others in the country'.[100] This was important work since the council courts relied as much on the suppression of litigation by compromise out of court or by the arbitration of individual councillors or local gentlemen as by judicial determination in the court itself.[101] With the consent of the parties and the lord chancellor, therefore, suits in star chamber were regularly committed to the hearing of local notables under the authority of writs of *dedimus potestatem*. Ellis supervised the joining of willing parties in commission and the naming of independent persons as commissioners, and drew the warrants for the writs of *dedimus potestatem*. While this method of procedure was rarely successful in stifling litigation, it could be useful as an economical way of taking evidence out of town. Indeed, in protracted suits it was often used solely for this purpose.

The activities of conciliar committees and individuals undoubtedly relieved the lord chancellor and the council in star
chamber of much trivial judicial work. The main deficiency in
this elementary form of curial organisation was precisely that
it was *ad hoc*. Evidence for the regnal year 17 Henry VIII establishes that a minimum of ninety-eight suits passed through
the machinery of star chamber during that year; for the year
20 Henry VIII, the figure is ninety-five suits; and for the last
six months of the cardinal's chancellorship, which fell within
the regnal year 21 Henry VIII, the total is a minimum of six-
ty-one suits. [102] This annual level of litigation, of compelling
magnitude even if the figures were realistic maxima rather
than minima, demanded a court which was professionally
organised and bureaucratised; demanded, too, that an act of
reform should achieve continuity of curial membership, in
place of fluidity, and should simultaneously resolve how far the
complex and already formalised procedure of star chamber
required the personal consideration of the king's councillors.

OUTSIDE STAR CHAMBER

By the time of Wolsey's supremacy, the self-styled description
'the king's most honourable council', as it then applied to the
councillors who performed the judicial work of the council outside star chamber, had become somewhat anachronistic. [103]
This was because the council attendant on Henry VIII, composed of those councillors who followed the royal court, advised the king and dealt with such suitors as appeared before
them, never recovered the degree of institutional embodiment
which the councillors attendant on Henry VII had possessed.
After the accession of Henry VIII, when both demand for conciliar justice and the organised facilities provided for it perhaps declined, such suitors who appeared in person where
the king was, found the late medieval practice in operation by
which the councillors who travelled with the royal court dealt

with bills of complaint as the need arose. By long tradition, the
dean of the chapel royal of the household and the king's
almoner were prominent in this work. When Wolsey was appointed lord chancellor, these two offices were held respectively by John Vesey and Richard Rawlyns. [104] Assistants to Vesey
and Rawlyns in their duties were Dr Edward Higgons, dean of
Shrewsbury and a master in chancery, John Gylberd, Thomas
Dalby, archdeacon of Richmond and provost of Beverley, and
Thomas Magnus, then a royal chaplain and archdeacon of
East Riding. [105]

It was not long before the effects of Wosley's ordering of the
judicial work of the council were felt by the dean and his
associates. The initial development in conciliar business outside star chamber was caused by an early decision to relieve
pressure on the council at Westminster by the transference of
minor civil suits to the hearing of the dean of the chapel royal *et
aliis de consilio.* [106] A large number of suits were so referred *ex
mandato domini cardinalis* and these were dealt with by the existing group of councillors who sat where the king was, following the royal progress. [107] Soon, however, further measures
were necessitated by the inability of Wolsey and the council in
star chamber to deal with the pressure of litigation and the
three orders of 1517, 1518 and 1520 established a series of temporary tribunals, staffed by councillors, for the hearing and expedition of poor men's causes. [108] These 'under-courts', as they
were known, were to sit in the palace of Westminster for the
convenience of suitors but were formally hived off from star
chamber. They were thus a novelty, as Wolsey's critics were
swift to observe, since they were sedentary council courts, but
outside the *camera stellata,* and not directed by the dean of the
chapel and his associates. Indeed the orders must be seen as
tantamount to an attempt to put much of the jurisdiction of the
council into commission, an expedient always dear to Wolsey's
heart, [109] since the definition of 'poor men' should be inter-
preted as liberally in the mouth of the minister as it was in
practice by the council and by litigants in the council
courts. [110]

The first order was pronounced by Wolsey on 18 June

1517;[111] the second on 17 June 1518.[112] Members of both the
resulting committees were John Islip, abbot of Westminster,
John Colet, dean of St Paul's, Sir Thomas Neville, Sir Andrew
Windsor, Dr John Clerk and William Roper. Sir Richard
Weston was appointed only in 1517; Robert Toneys, a busy
clerk in chancery and servant of Wolsey, was appointed only in
1518. The third order was dated 24 October 1520.[113] This
established a committee which consisted of Thomas Docwra,
prior of St John, John Bourchier lord Berners, Sir John Husye,
Sir John Pecche, Sir Weston Browne, Sir John Daunce, Sir
Henry Wyatt, William Ellis and William Ruddall. The 1520
group was probably the strongest on paper, since it comprised
most of the councillors then identified both with existing committee work and with reference, compromise and arbitration in
litigation current in star chamber. Nevertheless, the under-
courts in the white hall and elsewhere in the palace of Westminster proved a failure. Hall observed that much delay was
used and few matters ended.[114] A document in the case of Joan
Broke against Harry Bradbury is rather more informative, at
least in respect of the first two courts: it states that the abbot of
Westminster and his associates, to whom the matter had been
referred, had simply taken no action in the cases committed to
them.[115] The cardinal had overestimated the enthusiasm for
popular justice of the councillors appointed as members of the
tribunals of expedition. The men appointed were already
much troubled with the bills of litigants in their capacities as
councillors and also as arbitrators and umpires appointed by
Wolsey. Moreover, men of learning and experience could surely be excused their frustration with parties who, having paid
their fees of admission into court, treated litigation as a game
of chance.

   As in Joan Broke's case and others, the business which the
under-courts had failed to complete was therefore referred
once more to the dean of the chapel *et aliis de consilio.*[116] By the
year 1520, changes in personnel and additions had revised the
list of councillors particularly associated with this species of
activity to the following: Dr John Clerk, dean of the chapel
royal of the household (from 1519), Richard Rawlyns, king's

almoner, John Vesey, bishop of Exeter (from 1519), John Gylberd, Dr Roger Lupton, clerk of the hanaper and provost of Eton, Dr John Longland, dean of Salisbury, Dr John Stokesley and Sir Thomas More.[117] The increased workload faced by this new group of councillors was immediately reflected in their organisation and timetabling. The greatest change (from 1519) was of venue. The 'king's most honourable Council in his Court of Requests', as entries in the *acta* of these councillors styled the group in and after November 1520,[118] became a primarily sedentary body, keeping the law terms with new-found regularity in the white hall,[119] and only rarely moving to join the royal progress when the presence of all available personnel was required with the king's court.[120] The defendant who on 12 May 1523 turned up literally *ubicunque,* as was required in his writ, found himself in the wrong place, and notification of his appearance at the royal court on the set date had to be transmitted to the council in the white hall at Westminster.[121] When a departure from London was seen by the council as impending, a circumstance of increasing rarity, the parties in current litigation were ordered to make their future appearance at the places fixed. Thus on 21 February 1523, a defendant was ordered by the councillors in the white hall to make his next appearance before them four days later at Greenwich.[122] The establishment of the sedentary court, however, placed unrealistic demands on the time of the dean of the chapel of the household, whose official duties in the chapel royal were discharged on progress. After 1521, therefore, the newly appointed bishop of Lincoln, John Longland, may be found taking a prominent part on the bench at the white hall.

To compensate for the lack of facilities which suitors would otherwise have found for their causes where the king lay, a point on which Henry VIII had views since he felt that Wolsey left him with an insufficient council of his own,[123] two councillors were appointed to travel with the royal court. Dr Richard Wolman and Thomas Englefield, the two initially selected for the positions, followed the king's progress and discharged the former judicial functions of the council attendant, despatching business as required in and out of term, appointing arbitrators, arranging compromise out of court and maintaining constant liaison with the council in London. [124] These two councillors operated entirely within the orbit of the royal household, unlike, formerly, the dean of the chapel and the almoner who had worked within the council attendant. As, therefore, they could not readily avail themselves of the bureaucratic and secretarial processes of the privy seal, the standard procedural usage of the old council attendant and the councillors in the white hall, Wolman and Englefield reverted to the method adopted in the reign of Henry VII by Thomas Savage,[125] requiring the clerks of the signet to compose documents which served as writs of summons, commissions and orders.[126] These were sealed with the signet seal by the king's secretary and were known as 'letters missive'.[127] The royal sign manual, strictly necessary on such documents, was provided by means of a wooden stamp. In addition to Wolman and Englefield, other councillors resident in the king's household were called upon to assist in judicial work. Thus, early in 1521, the councillors in the white hall received notification that a current case had surceased: it had already been determined by Sir Thomas More 'in Curia domini Regis apud Grenewiche'.[128]

Soon, however, at the white hall as in star chamber there was a need for the despatch of much routine business out of court, especially the issue of procedural orders and rules by consent, the issue of process and commissions, the appointment of arbitrators, and the taking of recognisances. To fulfil this requirement, mainly accomplished in star chamber by William Ellis, Dr John Stokesley sat alone either in the white hall or in St Stephen's chapel at Westminster from 1521.[129] And like Ellis, Stokesley was also used by his colleagues as a specialist umpire, at which he appears at first sight to have worked effectively, determining a considerable number of suits despite Hall's quip that he was a better academic than a judge.[130] In his duty Stokesley was unlike John Kite, bishop of Carlisle and a former subdean, and the ubiquitous John Islip, abbot of Westminster, who were also appointed standing commissioners for the compromise of litigation but who again failed to act.[131] However, diligence and efficiency were not enough. The demise of Stokesley as a secular judge, in January 1523, appears to have been brought about by the hostility of the legal profession to the principles on which the learned doctor's decisions were given, especially in real property cases.[132] Wolsey was obliged to appoint a committee of inquiry, consisting of John Fitzjames, chief baron of the exchequer, Sir Richard Broke, Sir Anthony Fitzherbert, Sir Thomas More, Sir Robert Drury, William Wotton, second baron of the exchequer, and Thomas Englefield and John Porte, sergeants-at-law, 'to examine such causes as Mr. Stockesly hath given Judgement in the White hall and to make report whither they bee allowable or not'.[133] The committee reported, and Stokesley 'was deposid hys office'.[134] Hall therefore had the last laugh.

PROJECTED REFORM

These arrangements in star chamber and outside it were greatly *ad hoc* and by the mid-1520s the council and the council courts were in need of more lasting reform. The immediate requirement was surely that the council, if it was not to be divided into its administrative and judicial components, should be so reduced in size that it could as an institution possess the professionalism and regularity that would only come with a fixed and limited composition and a firm continuity of membership. It was also essential that an act of reform should establish the status and 'standing orders' of the conciliar courts. Reform was projected by Wolsey in 1525/6. First, in response to Henry VIII's protests that Wolsey was concentrating the king's council about his own person in London and leaving his master destitute of the councillors appropriate to his station as a leading Renaissance monarch, the Eltham Ordinances, published in January 1526, included the proposal for a reduced council of twenty members within the larger body which was to attend upon the king and resume the administrative and judicial work of the old council attendant.[135]

It would, however, be more correct to say (as Elton does) that this ordinance recorded Wolsey's final victory over the king's wish for a true council of his own. [136] The twenty 'honourable, virtuous, sadd, wise, experte, and discreete persons' who were to compose this council were the principal officers of state, leading civil servants and officials of the household, the bishops of Bath and Lincoln, and the dean of the chapel and Dr Wolman — the last pair clearly indicating Wolsey's continued resolve to maintain an undifferentiated council in which administration was intermingled with justice. However, by allowing the necessary absence in London of the important office-holders, the minister reduced this council for practical purposes to a committee of ten and then to a subcommittee of four, it being finally provided that two councillors at least from amongst those resident in the household should be always present to advise the king and to direct matters of justice: 'which direction well observed, the King's highnesse shall alwayes be well furnished of an honourable presence of councillors about his Grace, as to his high honour doth apperteyne'. [137] Such phraseology was, of course, richly ironic.

Nothing came of this idea during Wolsey's years in office, which was perhaps intentional, although within a decade it had formed the basis of Thomas Cromwell's reconstruction of the council. [138] A second plan, which was sketched out shortly afterwards in February 1526, was more realistic but equally abortive. [139] The proposal was for 'the devision of such maters as shalbe treated by the kinges Councell'. Wolsey therefore had moved to a new position and now favoured reform by differentiation, intending to relieve the principal office-holders and leading councillors of the council's judicial work. Twenty-eight named lesser councillors, together with 'the residue of the judges', 'the remnaunt of the barons of theschequyer', the attorney-general and sergeants-at-law were to be appointed to deal with 'mater in lawe'. [140] However, whether the twenty-eight were to constitute a single standing committee of councillors or several *ad hoc* committees to be nominated at the cardinal's future discretion is not clear. Nor is it apparent whether they were to become 'councillors at large' (to use the term of the later 1530s), excluded from the executive 'inner' council and retained only for justice, or to remain full members of an undivided king's council merely specialising in the judicial component of conciliar work.

In the event, again nothing resulted, and after three months' further consideration, Wolsey summoned seventeen councillors into star chamber on 15 May 1526 to resolve what was to be done.[141] Those present were fully representative of the judicial activity of the undivided council in star chamber, the white hall and elsewhere. The policy collectively decided on was that of the wholesale delegation of suits currently depending in the council courts in London to commissioners or to the provincial councils.

> It is to be noted that all the matters commensed this Terme of Easter afore this daye not committed being within the sheires herafter followinge be this daye orderid and decreed to be committed and directed to the Commissioners hereafter named of every Sheire or twoe of them to here and finallye to determyne the same matters.[142]

Standing commissioners were appointed for the English shires, almost certainly from stock lists already held in chancery, to deal with the cases committed to them.

> And yt is further orderid that all matters commensed here, beinge within the Sheires allotted to be determyned by my Ladye Princes Councell, to be committed to them. And semblable order is made for matters commensed here beinge within the Duke of Richmondes lymyttes of his Commission.[143]

Cases which originated in North Wales, South Wales and the marches were to be committed 'with the originall bokes therof' to the Princess Mary's council.[144] Those arising from Yorkshire, Cumberland, Westmorland and Northumberland were to be committed to the duke of Richmond's council in the north.[145] The first part of the policy, the issue of commissions to hear and end current suits, was undoubtedly a failure. It was an accepted procedure in the council courts that parties joined in commission only by mutual consent and with the permission of the court.[146] A few *ex parte* commissions were known, both in star chamber and the white hall, but these

were confined to cases where the plaintiff preferred the mediation of local gentlemen to the summoning of the defendant to
London.[147] Mandatory commissions were unworkable, since it
was the attitude and conduct of the litigants themselves which
determined the success or failure of the method. In many
cases, the parties simply obstructed all proceedings taken out
of town and demanded remission to London.[148] Nor could
commissions to hear and end succeed if either side obstinately
refused to settle, and in these cases the commissioners had no
alternative but to refer suits back to Westminster.[149] The
second part of the policy, the delegation of suits to the provincial councils, was new only in its scale. On 6 June 1519 the cardinal had ordered 'all matters within the power of the Commission in the Marches of Wales ... to be determined
there'.[150] On 21 June 1521 a similar order required 'all matters
of Cheshyre dependinge here [to be] remitted to the Counsell
in the Marches of Wales'.[151] But the remission of cases to the
provincial councils was not an effective method of determining
litigation. Many suits which were decided or dismissed in the
provinces resumed again in London, either after so-called new
evidence had turned up, or because the unsuccessful parties
refused to obey the decrees in their cases.[152] Wolsey's order
must have afforded the council courts no more than partial
relief, and the suggestion is that, despite proclamation of the
measure in Westminster hall and in Wales and the marches,
the practical effects were negligible.[153]

On 13 February 1527 the cardinal's policy of delegation was
firmly reiterated before the council in star chamber. It was also
embellished. All 'minute causes' depending 'as well yn thys
cort as yn all oder the kynges cortes' were to be remitted to the
assize judges and their associates on the bench for determination on circuit; 'and such matters as can not be determyned yn
their circute, the saide Justices and oder to determyn it if they
can at their owne houses'.[154] Unfortunately, no evidence as to
the nature of the 'minute' litigation in question, the extent of
its remission to the circuit judges and the effectiveness of its
determination by them can be discovered. The suspicion is
that in speaking of 'minute' cases the minister intended to

tackle the problem created by a growing band of litigants who insisted on wasting the council's time. Frivolous suitors, and their promoters and advisers, were the last of all persons to be deterred by the current policy. Their object was to tie up their opponents in a lengthy bout of litigation: not to win or end a case, but to avoid losing. Wolsey may have planned to subject the complaints of these suitors to the rigour of expert opinion locally. If so, however, the idea appears to have been dropped or proved impractical. This was a failure which was far from unique: no Tudor chancellor seemed able to devise a deterrent to the abuse of legal procedure more sophisticated than the threat of imprisonment or fine, public humiliation or a flogging.

Wolsey did not revive his earlier projects for the reform of the council. Nor was this surprising, as 1527 was the year in which the king's matrimonial scruples began to call earnestly upon the time and abilities of the minister. There were no further changes made in the management of star chamber prior to the cardinal's disgrace. Developments in the white hall were confined to a change and enlargement of personnel, perhaps combined with the provision of more effective and better defined curial organisation after the dismissal of Dr Stokesley.[155] Early in 1529 the clerk of the council in the white hall was to be found entering in his register 'the Names of suche Counsaillors as be appoynted for the herying of power Mennes causes in the kynges Courte of Requestes'.[156] The entry did not distinguish change in the institutional status of the councillors any more than had the earlier references to a 'court of requests' in 1520. The phrase identified their venue alone. Fifteen councillors were nominated, headed by John Longland, bishop of Lincoln, Richard Sampson, dean of the chapel, and Dr Wolman,[157] and thereafter all of them were to be found at work in the white hall, sometimes in groups and sometimes alone, sitting three or four times a week during the law terms.[158] At the fall of Wolsey, therefore, the integrity of the large, undivided king's council as an executive body and as two sedentary courts was maintained intact, a position which was to be held firm until 1536. The continuing *raison d'être* of the unreformed council under Sir Thomas More was probably its importance as a vehicle of consultation between the crown, the leading office-holders and those politically active and ambitious persons who were members of it. Ultimately, however, such a system could not be regarded as efficient.

3

Star Chamber Matter

PRIVATE SUITS

The council in star chamber under Wolsey became increasingly developed as a court of the realm in which litigation was
conducted between private parties. Eight hundred and twenty-one cases between party and party with proceedings extant
in the present star chamber archive can be dated to the years of
the cardinal's chancellorship. To these suits must be added
213 dated cases without extant proceedings, discovered in the
Ellesmere extracts, Hudson's notes and other sources.[1]
Another 651 cases with proceedings may also belong to the
period, but definite dates cannot be assigned to the
documents.[2] The number of star chamber cases between
private parties during Wolsey's ascendancy may thus have
been as high as 1,685. In the interests of substantive if not
quantitative accuracy, however, present discussion of the
litigation heard in star chamber under Wolsey has been
restricted to definite cases.

During Wolsey's supremacy, the subject-matter of private
litigation before the council in star chamber came to fall into
five areas. The first and largest category consisted of riot, rout,

unlawful assembly, forcible entry, assault, trespass and related offences, generally in cases where the possession of real property or chattels was in question. It is clear, when it is possible to get at pleadings other than bills of complaint, that title is doubly more frequent as the real issue in this area than all the alleged crimes of violence put together. The second category took in maintenance and champerty, corrupt verdicts by juries, embracery, perjury and subornation, abuse of legal procedure and other offences prejudicial to public justice, and crimes unpunished at common law. The third comprised cases of the corruption of royal and franchisal officers. The fourth encompassed municipal and trade disputes. The fifth area, while essentially miscellaneous, derived some coherence from the actual or potential violence alleged by most plaintiffs in their bills, although in circumstances other than those of the first category of offences. The real subjects in this last area, which ranged from crimes and torts to unsocial acts and civil disputes, were evident from the complaints, but were often laced with exaggerated charges of public or domestic disorder. The range of the subject-matter of private litigation is best illustrated by a table. Sufficiency of documentation makes it possible to discover the principal 'real' matter behind 473 of the dated Wolsey cases. Table 1 presents the distribution of these cases by subject within the five categories.

Table 1

Category and Subject	Distribution of cases
I	
Riot, rout, unlawful assembly	35
Forcible entry, dispossession, forcible detainder	4
Assault, battery, false imprisonment	11
Trespass to chattels, detinue, conversion, illegal distress	48
Title	194

II

Maintenance, champerty	6
Corrupt verdict	5
Embracery, perjury, subornation	5
Abuse of legal procedure	10
Felony unpunished, being accessary to felony, 'bearing' of felons, rescue of felons	12
Contempt of decree in earlier star chamber suit	6

III

Officers' malfeasance	28

IV

Municipal dispute	8
Trade dispute (except engrossing, forestalling, regrating)	6
Engrossing, forestalling, regrating	3

V

Breach of contract	5
Debt	11
Defamation	3
Easements dispute	10
Enclosure dispute	17
Extortion, embezzlement (except by officers)	3
Forgery	5
Fraud	3
Hunting offence	6
Interruption of family relations	5
Landlord and tenant, rent dispute	10
Nuisance	2
Testamentary dispute	4
Tithes dispute	8
Total	473

Two-thirds of the suits within the first category which complained of riotous and violent demeanour were in reality about unquiet titles. The cases were the 'English bill' equivalents of actions of trespass *quare clausum fregit* and actions on the statutes of forcible entry at common law.[3] The root of legal title to freehold was seisin.[4] Seisin, however, was a relative concept. In the thirteenth century, it took a minimum of four days for a disseisor to become seised as against the disseisee, and in the interim period the disseisee had a right of entry. By the fourteenth century, the right of entry of the disseisee endured until it was 'tolled', usually in the event of a 'descent cast'. Disseisin as a result came to mean 'where a man entreth into any lands or tenements where his entry is not congeable, and ousteth him that hath the freehold'.[5] Increasingly claimants were advised by their lawyers to make an entry. As Milsom observes, the tenant could accept this, go out, and himself bring novel disseisin; but normally he would resist and put the claimant out. If the claimant's entry was not a disseisin, it followed that he himself became seised thereby and that to put him out was to disseise him.[6] All this opened the way for a certain amount of self-help, and as a preventative measure against potential disorders there began in 1381 a series of statutes prohibiting forcible entry, even if the claimant had a right to enter.[7] During the fifteenth century, lawyers devised an alternative method of approach. Since forcible entry was illegal, peaceful entries on possession were made, usually followed by damage to property, with the intention of drawing-on actions of trespass *quare clausum fregit* by which title could be tried. Using the appropriate pleading, an alleged trespasser justified his entry and the question of title arose which the court would have to determine. This was the position in Wolsey's day, since the action of *ejectio firmae* did not become used for the trial of freehold titles until the third quarter of the sixteenth century.[8]

It was natural that the real or fictitious entries, ousters, and damage necessary to the mechanism for claiming land at law should be translated into the bills of complaint of plaintiffs in the council courts. Litigants and their lawyers devised such charges to invite the attention of the court to which they addressed themselves, and to elevate their cases to the domain of royal jurisdiction, and beyond the claims of the local courts.

Lawyers were also well aware that allegations of riot and forcible entry, violence and intimidation, were particularly suited to the construction of star chamber matter in view of the council's traditional association with disruptions of public order. Many tenants, when ousted by a claimant, preferred a bill in star chamber to an action at law.[9] The procedural advantages were considerable. Litigation over titles, however, was rarely straightforward. Claimants who mustered a following and entered, but were repulsed by tenants and their servants, alleged in star chamber – after the former fashion of novel disseisin – that they themselves had been put out by armies of 'riotous persons' while each respectively was 'seised in his demesne as of freehold'.[10] With well drawn pleadings and careful management, such a suit by a claimant could put his opponent to much trouble. The method was especially inconvenient if the tenant had an action in progress against him at common law, and a bill in star chamber was often in retaliation to other litigation.[11]

The possibilities for an experienced litigant were considerable. One illustration will suffice.[12] Early in Wolsey's chancellorship, John Dodd became 'seised in his demesne as of fee' by inheritance of forty acres of land in Shropshire. However, about 1525, Thomas Shelton made a claim for the moiety of the land on the grounds that he was co-parcener with Dodd. Shelton began a suit in chancery, and demanded that Dodd produce his deeds for inspection. Dodd appeared to file his answer, but the case dragged on and was still depending three years later. Shelton, meanwhile, started a second suit before the council in Wales, but was remitted to the common law. As a result, he commenced an action in the court of common pleas. Dodd made his appearance by attorney in Hilary term 1527, and again Shelton failed to obtain a result. Litigation had not proved fruitful as far as the claimant was concerned. In consequence, on 26 November 1527 Shelton made an entry *vi et armis* and interfered with Dodd's livestock; but the tenant was not to be drawn, and no action at law resulted. . Clearly short of money for expenditure on lawyers' fees himself, Shelton at this point sold his title to George Bromley, a Shropshire justice of the peace and learned counsel to the council in Wales. Shelton averred that if Bromley so troubled Dodd by vexatious litigation, using his influence to advantage, Dodd would be obliged to cut his losses and sell out cheaply. Thus, to facilitate future suits, Bromley gathered an armed mob and made an entry on 2 January 1528, as he himself later claimed, 'to execute livery and seisin of and upon the feoffment'. In his subsequent account, however, the armed following were supposedly friends acting as 'witnesses'. Bromley, after the events of 2 January, then claimed to be 'seised in his demesne as of fee' of the moiety of the land, and procured Shelton to file a bill before the council in Wales alleging a riot by Dodd. The tenant was summoned to answer, and the case was dismissed. The dismission was followed by further entries, and these finally provoked Dodd into filing a bill in star chamber. Wolsey's policy at this time was to remit to the provincial councils all suits arising within the limits of their commissions, and the cardinal revealed his keen sense of justice in Dodd's case by sending a personal letter to the council in Wales, advising them to 'seperate the said Bromley from you that be Counsailors, not making hym privey to any maner of processe, examynacion or consultacion, but onely as a partie and suter bifore you in this mater'.[13] Thereafter, the case unfortunately disappears from the record, although it was undoubtedly referred back to Westminster, since the extant proceedings are to be found in the present star chamber archive.

In the majority of suits within the first area of star chamber matter which concerned disputed titles, the acts of violence alleged by plaintiffs against their opponents were exaggerated or fictitious, and of secondary importance only. The parties had come to star chamber to argue about their respective rights to real or personal property. It should be emphasised that many suitors were not interested in a final hearing and judicial determination of their claims. An outstanding procedural attraction of the council courts, much developed by Wolsey in star chamber, was the availability of arbitration and equitable compromise.[14]   The   advantage   of   pursuing settlements of this type was that the tenor of an award devised by mediators and accepted by the parties could be entered as of record in the registers of the council, and could be deemed enforceable by conciliar process. Sometimes, however, judicial determination was really required, and star chamber would usually provide it, the lord chancellor calling upon the expert advice of the chief or puisne justices who attended the council. These legal opinions formed the basis of the council's subsequent decrees.[15] Nevertheless, the council would not always proceed at the suit of the party. A few plaintiffs were non-suited or dismissed to common law at an early stage;[16] they were probably suspected time-wasters. On other occasions, the council heard the 'riot' but left the title.[17] On the other hand, it was the council itself which appears to have felt it desirable in a number of cases to attempt the judicial hearing of a much disputed title, or that a pretended title should be silenced.[18] How far litigants were prepared to co-operate in such circumstances is doubtful: the extant proceedings emphasise that litigants would not proceed if the way seemed unfavourable to their interests.

While the loss of the Henrician council registers imposes limitations on general statements, there can be no doubt that, under Wolsey and throughout the reign of Henry VIII, the council in star chamber 'dealt with titles' as mediator or judge, and 'settled possessions'.[19] Many instances survive in which a title was scrutinised before the council, found good and confirmed, and the appropriate orders were made for possession.[20] Thus, late in 1519 or early in 1520, the council decreed in favour of John Warde's title to a parcel of land in Lillingstone Lovell in Oxfordshire, and made an order for the restitution of possession and profits against Nicholas Wentworth.[21] On 1 February 1526, Wolsey pronounced a decree for John Haselwood's right to the manor of Maidwell in Northamptonshire.[22] In a case which began under Wolsey and was ended in 1530 by Sir Thomas More, Elizabeth Holdforde successfully sued for the recovery of her jointure. Her opponent was commanded to permit Elizabeth and her second husband to possess lands, rents and 'other commodities', according to an indenture 'shewed into this Court'.[23] When Elizabeth later complained that the full effect of the decree was denied to her, the council ordered the reappearance of the defendant by writ of *subpoena* to make answer.[24] The council under successive lord chancellors maintained its position on title without interruption until the 1550s. The reversal of policy began in October 1551, following a government decision – pronounced in star chamber – that the council courts were no longer to entertain litigation to the 'derogation' of the common law.[25] Star chamber practice within a decade was clear and, with rare exceptions, uniformly observed.[26] The court did not touch unquiet titles, which were referred to the determination of common law;[27] nor did it 'meddle' with possession, 'except that if the partie be put forth of possession by a ryot or such unlawfull act, in that case the court wold reastore him as he was, before the same unlawfull act comytted'.[28]

Not all the alleged acts of violence in the first area of star chamber's activity were fictitious or exaggerated. Genuine complaints of trespass and assault brought before Wolsey included those of a number of tenants for years seeking recovery of their terms.[29] The termor in the sixteenth century was well protected at common law, but his chances of success there were not great against a lessor who had raided his tenant's house and destroyed the documents inside.[30] Some major disturbances were also brought to the attention of the council in star chamber.[31] Wolsey had declared to Henry VIII that his intention was to punish riotous persons and their procurers 'that they shalbi war howe from thes forth they shall redres ther mater with ther handes'.[32] The elements of riot had been defined before the council on 24 November 1488. The statement, while it no doubt represented existing practice, became the basis of star chamber's position in the late fifteenth and sixteenth centuries. Riots were effected by a company of three or more, assembling and forcibly attempting the unlawful act which they intended.[33] Riot, as a result of its definition, became the most frequently alleged offence in the first area of business, since if the 'wonted number' were present, the smallest of encounters might be 'made a riot' by a plaintiff who knew the form.[34] Nevertheless, analysis establishes that in some cases riot was a real principal or supplementary issue. The council dealt severely with those defendants who confessed or were convicted,[35] and no differentiation was made between procurers of riot and actual rioters.[36] On 22 June 1516, the abbot of Dieulacres was fined for riot in the course of a dispute about land and its profits.[37] Dr John Jenyn, president of Queens' College in Cambridge, was examined on 30 November 1526 concerning riots committed during his two-year quarrel with the fellows over the president's emoluments and expenses.[38] The case was taken into star chamber after Simon Heynes and four other fellows had made suit to Wolsey and the council by bill of complaint.[39] The outcome of Jenyn's examination is not clear; however, within six months he had been deposed and Heynes had succeeded as president.[40]

In cases where three persons were not involved, or in lesser matters, the plaintiff, in consultation with his counsel, was obliged to fall back on forcible entry, assault, or some form of trespass, whichever best suited his requirements. On 19 May 1519 Richard Coryton was imprisoned for a forcible entry in support of his title;[41] on 16 November 1528, William Harrys was similarly dealt with upon confession of unlawful assembly in his answer.[42] But most suits were trivial. An allegation of forcible entry and seizure of cattle turned out to be a claim for £1 3s 4d paid to a bailiff as rent in advance for a field which was subsequently secured by the defendant.[43] Other so-called forcible entries were in reality disputes about straying sheep.[44] A further case was about some lead which vanished from a roof.[45] No matter, seemingly, was too small for the attenton of the king's councillors. Sometimes more serious were suits alleging trespass to chattels, detinue, conversion or illegal distress, and a number of supposed 'riots' turned out to fall within this class of offence. The amount at stake could be considerable. One plaintiff lost possession of 320 sheep, which were famished for three weeks before being returned to him. Even then, six score were missing, having been converted to mutton 'contrary to law, right, and good conscience'.[46]

The second area of business took in all offences prejudicial to law enforcement and public justice, and included notorious crimes which remained unpunished at common law. Wolsey had announced his enforcement policy in his oration of 2 May 1516, and there was no shortage of scope for its practical execution. Something of the local situation in Leicestershire, for example, was defined in affairs between Thomas Grey, marquis of Dorset, and Sir Richard Sacheverell.[47] As we have seen, informations had been filed in king's bench against these and other councillors in 1516.[48] The judges held back, knowing that the king would decide what was to be done. What happened was that the offenders were given a serious fright and were then commanded to 'diligently applie theymselfes for thadministracion of indifferent justice'.[49] Since 1511, however, when Sacheverell had married Mary Hungerford, widow of Edward lord Hastings, he had 'used hymself in maner of comparison with the Lord marques; soo that the shire ever sithence hath been in grete division by mean of the same'.[50] Rivalry, inevitably, had run by 1525 to the perversion of due legal process at assizes and quarter sessions. Sacheverell's conduct and the number of his following at assizes in that year had so alarmed the justices, Sir Robert Brudenell and Sir Anthony Fitzherbert, that Sacheverell was ordered 'with his company' to 'avoid and depart'.[51] Perhaps the judges subsequently complained to Wolsey; certainly the marquis of Dorset filed his own private information. Evidence was taken. Sir William Skevington declared that when Sacheverell was absent, 'ther was moche better ordre and quiete at sessions and assises'.[52] Sir John Digby observed 'that justice ware well ministred in the absence of the said Sir Richard, and moche better then it hath been sithence his comying to the same'. Sacheverell had not come to the sessions and assizes to maintain 'indifferent justice': 'for he cometh with such a company that he ruleth the whole court'.[53] Digby claimed to have seen him arrive with a following of a hundred or more. Juries had also been tampered with. At Leicester assizes in late July 1525, John Gladwyn, 'an honest, indifferent man', was sworn as a juror and was at once informed of the arrangements made by Sacheverell for courts there. Gladwyn was unmoved, however, even by the presence of forty of Sir Richard's supporters; and when he overheard a servant warn one 'Nut', who attended on the jury, that he should 'take hede to Gladwyn, for he can pleye the[e] falss', Gladwyn himself retorted that it only became 'suche a fals knave as thow art full evill so to saye or so to enbrace any of the kinges Jury'.[54] Needless to say, Gladwyn was called as a witness before the council *ex parte* the marquis of Dorset. Later events are, unfortunately, unknown.

While the enforcement of the existing law in the courts of common law, not prosecution in star chamber, was the essence of Wolsey's scheme, the council was more than willing to receive complaints from private parties concerning 'enormities' contrary to public justice. Local influence and prejudice, maintenance and embracery, subornation and perjury, were alleged in most bills filed during Wolsey's chancellorship; although in only a handful of cases were maintenance, champerty, embracery, perjury or subornation the principal offences advanced by plaintiffs. Juries were hauled into star chamber for corrupt verdicts or perjury in 1516, 1517, 1520, 1523, 1527 and 1529.[55] In another suit of 1521, two members of an inquest filed a bill against three of their colleagues, alleging that the former had been 'sore menaced' with threat of bodily fear, 'by cause they wyll not fynde accordynge to the myndes of the said oder iij wilfull persons and theme that so labor theme'.[56] The defendants, motivated by maintenance and perjury 'contrary the trewthe, right and all good conscience', had procured unnecessary adjournments, and had achieved the removal of the inquest's venue by thirty miles and more. The council was also called upon to sort out muddles. In 1520 a grand jury of Sussex had failed to find a true bill against a gang charged with breaking a dovecote.[57] This was despite the fact that all but one of the accused, Elys Midmore, had confessed to the crime. The jury doubted the validity of the confessions. William Lowle, for example, could not have been involved 'accordyng as he hath surmysed and confessed before dyvers Justices', because six credible persons swore otherwise.

From this it followed that those who accused Lowle in their own confessions were 'forsworn' and were themselves 'of most likelihood' not there either. The confession of William Norles was similarly contradicted by other sworn evidence; and that of Robert Sage was of 'no credence' since 'he hath been rakyd in the Tower', as the jury were informed by the lieutenant of the Tower himself. This conflict of evidence left the jurors, as they said, unable to act. If they found a true bill, it would be against conscience, since 'substantial' evidence proved the accused 'not to be ther'; if they did not find the bill, the confessions were against them 'contrary to the lawe'. The jurors therefore resolved to make 'presentment' before the king's council.[58]

How this incident should be viewed is not clear. If the accused were looking for help from friends in court, only an act of God or an ingenious appeal in equity to the council could prevent the finding of a true bill. There was, however, no doubt as to the council's reaction. The matter was heard in star chamber on 30 January 1521. Elys Midmore, who had not confessed, was examined on oath and denied the charges. But the council believed the existing confessions, which were presented for inspection, and Wolsey declared Midmore 'convict of the said offence aswell as of perjurye for his denyenge of the same'.[59] Even so, the council may possibly have been more naive than the original grand jury. After his condemnation by the cardinal, Midmore with an iron nerve accused Thomas Fiennes, lord Dacre, of promoting the suit of malice and procuring the confessions.[60] This was a sentiment shared by four of Midmore's associates; and it was true that Fiennes had presided over the confession of Robert Sage, and therefore by implication over the racking in the Tower.[61] Moreover, the enthusiasm with which Fiennes subsequently began actions of *scandalum magnatum* against such insubstantial accusers in the court of common pleas gives grounds for suspicion.[62] Wolsey, however, was irritated rather than impressed and 'for the which sclaunderinge of the said Lorde, the same Midmore was adjudged to the Pillorye'.[63] The case was then referred back to Sussex, the grand jurors, who may also have been brought before the council, having 'agreid to aferme the whole bill' against the accused, excepting only the charge against one Edmund Bocher who had a cast-iron alibi.[64] Nevertheless, the jury's affirmation did not end the council's interest. The following April, the duly found bills of indictment were scrutinised by the council and were formally handed to Thomas Fiennes and John Carell (a sergeant-at-law), who were no doubt to ensure that no mistakes were made in getting convictions.[65] Undoubtedly, here was an area being charted for the future star chamber. The episode of the Sussex jury represented the intervention of the council in a primarily executive capacity; perhaps wrongly, it has not been counted as a star chamber 'case'. The lack of differentiation between the executive and judicial operations of the Henrician council can sometimes be striking, for while the council treated this jury's inability to act as an essentially administrative problem, it was addressed by the jurors as a 'court'[66] and the council did indeed judge the strength of the evidence against the accused. Lord chancellors after Wolsey saw the need to maintain the development of conciliar jurisdiction in this important field. Notably, by the reign of Edward VI, the council's role included the regular official prosecution of corrupt juries in star chamber.[67] The efficacy of this work was in turn enhanced by the strength of star chamber's contribution to the definition of legal doctrine.[68]

The council under Wolsey also developed control over the abuse of legal procedure by vexatious litigants and the maintainers of unnecessary suits, both in star chamber and at common law.[69] Those convicted of such offences would be compelled to reimburse the legal expenses of the parties whom they had injured, and were given appropriate punishment. Anthony Malorye was committed to the Fleet in 1525 for a frivolous suit in star chamber against Alexander Cundalle and others, and was ordered to pay their costs taxed by Wolsey at £6 13s 4d.[70] John Middlemore had been similarly dealt with in 1519, upon complaint that he had maliciously procured the false indictment of John Robinson for felony in the county of Worcester.[71] In 1527, upon the certificate of Sir Henry Grey

and Walter Luke that a bill of complaint referred to them was
untrue, Henry Taylor, the plaintiff, was imprisoned by the
council as a common barrator.[72] Several suitors in star
chamber made the abuse of legal procedure their principal
allegation, and ten undoubtedly had a case. More complaints
may also have been substantial, although litigants rarely failed
to regard cases against them in other courts as being wholly
unjustified.

At least twenty-one complaints were filed before the council
in star chamber during Wolsey's chancellorship which alleged
felony unpunished at common law because of technical
problems, the accessaries to felony, the 'bearers' of felons, or
the rescue of murderers. Sufficient additional evidence is extant to confirm the subject-matter of twelve of these suits. Of
the twenty-one bills, five concerned the indictment of
murderers.[73] Maintenance and collusion had prevented the
successful implementation of due legal process. Three plaintiffs charged defendants with being accessaries to murder.[74]
Another bill alleged that the defendant had poisoned the plaintiff's sister eight years previously, but the case seems to have
been a fabrication.[75] A widow complained of the murder of her
husband, the former captain of Norham castle. The crime had
been committed in Scotland, and the murderers could not
therefore be indicted at law.[76] Two rescues of murderers were
reported by the relatives of the deceased.[77] Six suits concerned
notorious and unpunished abductions and rape.[78] On 2 June
1524 Sir Robert Constable was obliged to kneel upon the
quadrangle in star chamber, 'for takinge awaye Anne Grisacre
the kinges warde, and afficiancinge her to his sonne Thomas,
and suffringe hym before mariage to know her Carnally'. The
defendant was humbled before the presence; and, placing
himself in the king's mercy, submitted to whatever fines should
be assessed for his offences.[79] Of the remaining bills, a case of
robbery of a church was remitted to the common law,[80] a
so-called murder turned out to be a tithes dispute,[81] and
allegations of housebreaking and rape proved to be a frivolous
suit.[82] Examination of the twelve better documented cases indicates that Wolsey's policy was to consolidate traditional con-

ciliar practice. The council in star chamber heard serious crimes at the suit of private parties, and in exceptional circumstances tried felonies, which it punished as misdemeanours.[83] But the council would always remit cases for trial at law, if the balance of probabilities favoured a successful conviction by due process. This was the council's usual procedure when it was called upon to investigate crime and untangle technicalities in its executive capacity,[84] and it would so act despite special pleading by the accused that he could not enjoy an impartial trial in his locality.[85]

As its judicial activities increased, the council went some way towards better enforcement of its own decrees by the strengthening of its contempt jurisdiction.[86] In civil suits, however, the council was entirely dependent on the litigants themselves for information. From time to time, plaintiffs in their bills alleged that the activities of defendants were contrary to an earlier decree of the council; in six cases, such contempt was the principal charge.[87] When contempts were reported, the council took action and, if necessary, fines or imprisonment would be ordered.[88] Performance of the decree, however, was another matter. While the council, under Wolsey's guidance, published its desire to suppress 'enormities' in the administration of justice, the question of the efficacy and enforcement of its own star chamber decrees proved to have no easy solution.

The third area of business was precisely defined. At least four cases of officers' malfeasance had been heard in star chamber at the suit of private parties in the reign of Henry VII,[89] and thirty-eight bills of complaint filed during Wolsey's chancellorship charged royal or franchisal officers with corruption or extortion. At least twenty-eight of these suits were in reality concerned with alleged malfeasance, and lack of documentation accounts for the remaining ten cases. Some suits were undoubtedly justified. In July 1516 an undersheriff was sent to the Fleet because he had distrained cattle for £5 and sold them for £15.[90] A bailiff was imprisoned in July 1519 for assessing unjust amercements on William Barnes.[91] Early in 1529 another bailiff was brought to account in star chamber for extortion and fraudulent conversion. [92]

But a number of suits against officers were frivolous. Richard Wharton, bailiff of Bungay in Suffolk, received more than his fair share of persecution at the hands of the tenants within his franchise. Matters began in 1515, when the inhabitants of Bungay complained to the council that Wharton and his friends had violated the local pageants out of 'wilful vexation'. [93] Wharton's answer was tantamount to a confession, but the matter was a trifle and it was revealed that the pageants were old and shortly to be replaced. Nevertheless, the plaintiffs were evidently successful, since thereafter the bailiff became the victim of a local crusade: eight lengthy suits began in star chamber in which Wharton and his assistant, John Gyrlyng, were defendants. [94] The eight plaintiffs, Rychars, Dowsyng, Fuller, Southall, Lynde, Coseler, Denham and Wace, alleged corruption, misfeasance, assault, trespass, illegal distress and the theft of two sheep. In retaliation, Wharton filed three bills against Rychars, Dowsyng and Fuller; and Gyrlyng filed a complaint against Southall. [95] After some years and a number of fruitless commissions, four of the suits came to hearing. [96] The cases brought by Rychars, Dowsyng and Southall were dismissed. Rychars's and Southall's suits were found to have been procured of malice, and both men were committed to the Fleet. [97] The outcome of the cases initiated by the others is unknown.

The deputy-constable of Conway castle was also the subject of a vexatious suit. [98] Roger Jenkynson, a burgess of the town, filed a bill of complaint addressed to Wolsey alleging that four years previously the deputy-constable, Thomas Salisbury, had equipped his servants with weapons offensive and defensive, and had forcibly entered Jenkynson's house, seizing goods and chattels worth £4 4s. The plaintiff claimed that Salisbury had detained the goods 'contrary to right', and when suit was made to the council in Wales the defendant had again raised a following and forcibly entered the house. Thereafter Salisbury was alleged to have imprisoned Jenkynson in the castle 'as a felon' for five weeks. The bill, complaining of matters four years past, evidently took the deputy-constable by surprise.

When the truth came out, however, it was revealed that the plaintiff and his associates had been involved in local disturbances, and six of them had been kept in ward in the castle for a week prior to being released on bail to appear at the sessions at Caernarvon. There can be no doubt that the provision of facilities for individuals to bring corruption, abuses, and private wrongs to the attention of the king's council was, in principle, praiseworthy. But judicial machinery which provided no rigorous procedure for the early elimination of frivolous suits could have no hope of efficient working in the absence of a more severe chancellor like Sir Thomas More or Sir Thomas Egerton.

The fourth category of business consisted of municipal and trade disputes. In the reign of Henry VII, eleven suits had been examined which concerned municipalities, trade and commerce.[99] This jurisdiction was appropriate to the council, since 'where good ordre lacketh and division be amongest any Comynaltie, there shall ensue desolacion and destruccion of thesame Cominaltie'.[100] During Wolsey's supremacy, a minimum of seventeen such cases came before the council in star chamber.[101] Eight cases related to municipalities or franchises. Three of these, however, owed little to the cardinal. Two suits about an election of aldermen at York were to be ended by More,[102] and a customs dispute between the town of Tewkesbury and the sheriffs of Bristol had not reached a hearing by 1530.[103] The proceedings in two of the remaining five cases are fragmentary. In 1520 the University of Oxford complained of the mayor's unreasonableness and unwillingness to settle out of court an existing suit for which no other proceedings are extant.[104] The city's grievance related to the University's failure to punish those of its members implicated in 'a heinous murder'. The second case was initiated by the mayor of Waterford, who filed a bill of complaint against the inhabitants of New Ross concerning the infringement of certain liberties and various acts of violence.[105] The results of these suits are not known.

The other three municipal suits are well documented. The mayor and aldermen of Newcastle's case against certain of the gild merchants of the town was ended on 2 May 1516, the same day as Wolsey's law-enforcement policy was declared to the king and council. [106] The matters in dispute in the town had led to 'grete commocions, unlaufull assembles, confederacies, embraceries, conventicles, unlaufull promyses and divisions in the same Towne'. [107] The real question, however, was the claim of the local craftsmen to 'occupy merchandise' by retailing commodities foreign to their trades. To counter the craftsmen's case, the trading gilds produced weighty evidence to the effect that 'no craftesman should occupy eny marchaundisez othir then for the necessary of their household and famylie'. [108] The council decided in favour of the trading gilds: no change from a craft to a trade gild might be made except upon renunciation of the craft gild. [109] This decree was to be exemplified under the great seal and openly proclaimed in Newcastle 'for a perpetual memory'.

William Dale's suit against the mayor and aldermen of Bristol began in 1519. [110] Dale had been elected a sheriff at Michaelmas 1518, and he complained to the council shortly afterwards about the financial impositions placed upon him 'for the Mayntenaunce and upholdyng of the Mairealtie, and payment of the Fees for other officers . . . as Recorder, Towne Clerke, Swordberer, attorney and other'. [111] The plaintiff supplied a detailed schedule of the objectionable charges. The mayor, in his answer, argued that the sheriffs 'have alweys paide and borne . . . the fees of the Maire and oder officers of the said towne and oder charges of olde tyme accustumed'. [112] The council examined Dale's schedule, and a new scale of charges appears to have been devised by Wolsey. At the chancellor's order, the mayor and aldermen assembled in the Guildhall at Bristol in October 1519, in moderation of charges 'before this time yearly sustained' by the sheriffs. [113] The new schedule modified the town's expenditure and restricted 'drinkings'. [114] Dale, however, received no personal redress, since his term of office had expired before the new rules came into effect.

The *cause célèbre* of the cardinal's chancellorship was the dispute between the prior and the city of Norwich. [115] The issues between the parties were of long standing and concerned their respective liberties: the prior insisted that the site of the priory, Holmstrete, Tombland, Raton-row and other places, were not within the jurisdiction of the city. The matter had been the source of controversy in Norwich in 1429, [116] and in 1442 the parties were before the council of Henry VI. [117] In 1491 the dispute had begun again in star chamber before the council of Henry VII. [118] This litigation, which 'occasioned a very large expense to both parties', [119] lasted for thirty-two years before the matter came to a final decree. Wolsey, as he himself put it, 'of his charitable disposicion travayled in his owne person for thexaminacion of the same matturs': the cardinal visited the site in Norwich, and caused a 'book' to be engrossed by the judges recording the jurisdictional interests of the parties and the points of agreement and disagreement. [120] The minister considered the 'book' and moved the mayor to persuade the city to concede; but the common assembly of Norwich was 'not in ony wyse aggreable'. [121] Wolsey then became impatient, and in late 1523 he imposed a composition on the contestants. Under this award, the city resigned all juridiction within the walls of the priory, the latter site being deemed to be part of the county of Norfolk, and the church gave up all rights of jurisdiction outside the walls of the priory and within the walls of the city. Holmstrete, Tombland and Raton-row were by Wolsey's order compulsorily alienated to the city, and the priory was exempted from tolls within Norwich. The city resigned to the church its rights of commonage in Eaton and Lakenham. The prior was obliged to convey to the citizens in fee a quantity of pasture, being part of this common, and six feet of ground round it in order that a ditch might enclose the land to the use of the poor inhabitants of the city. [122] When the parties inquired of the cardinal at whose expense the land should be drained, Wolsey, by this time wholly exasperated, ordered the ditch to be dug at his own personal expense. [123] The agreement was exemplified under the great seal in May 1524 and a final composition was sealed between the prior and the city at the Norwich Guildhall on 2 September following. [124]

Nine suits concerned trade and commerce. The cases

brought before the council ranged from restrictive practices
and the status of alien craftsmen in London, to the selling of
cloth and lead ore in the provinces.[125] The council in its
executive capacity was at all times concerned with economic
regulation, in particular with the prices of victuals and
manufactured goods, and the manipulation of grain supplies in
times of scarcity.[126] A number of engrossers, forestallers, and
regraters of grain were reported to the centre in 1520.[127] Two
cases were initiated in 1528 and 1529 respectively; these are of
interest since they were the only star chamber suits now extant
for the period of Wolsey's chancellorship which claimed to be
brought on a proclamation. The proclamation of 12 November
1527 had declared 'that no manner of person . . . do from
henceforth in any manner of wise regrate, forestall, or engross
any wheat or any other manner of grain'.[128] Commissioners
were appointed to survey 'barns, garners, ricks, and stacks',
and to compel those who possessed 'more corn than shall be
thought convenient by their discretions for the use of their
households and seed' to bring such excess grain to market for
sale.[129] William Barett's bill of complaint, which was filed early in 1528, alleged that 'the fyrst market day next ensuying
after the seyd proclamacyon so proclamyd, the seyd James
Newby havyng good plenty of grayne wold not send no part
ther of in to the market'.[130] According to Barett, the defendant
also ignored the subsequent commands of the king's commissioners. The case was undoubtedly brought on the
proclamation of the previous November: the draftsman had
appended a charge to officers to execute the statutes concerning vagabonds, beggars and unlawful games, and the plaintiff, not missing an opportunity, added to his bill that the
defendant was known 'for a commen gamener with Tabull
play and dyse and Cards'.[131] The complaint of the constables
of Yaxley, filed the following year, likewise declared that the
defendants had feared not 'the kinges gracious proclamacion
made against Forstallers, Regratours, and ingrocers of
corne'.[132] Thomas Alward and Christopher Branston were
alleged to have engrossed grain to such an extent that 'the said
grains' and 'peas and beans' rose in price by two shillings a

quarter within three market days. [133]

The final area of star chamber matter encompassed the remarkable range of private litigation not described in previous categories. While an essentially miscellaneous collection of cases defies rigid classification, a degree of homogeneity was provided by the allegations of actual or potential violence, and the threats to public or domestic order which were included to attract the attention of the council. Unlike the first category of business, where violence alone tended to be advanced in the bill of complaint and the title or other real issue was usually introduced in later pleadings, in the fifth area the real subject was apparent from the start. It was nevertheless concealed among statements which were often purely fictional, and the suspicion is that the practice was continued by litigants and lawyers under Wolsey, despite the greater availability of the council in star chamber for judicial work, to avoid the dismission by the chancellor of trivial civil suits to the dean of the chapel for hearing.

Many suits within the fifth area of business were indeed insignificant, and more have been rendered so by severe loss of documentation. Issues ranged from non-payment of small rents and an organ-builder's bad debts, [134] to seduction and enticement accompanied by an alleged attempted poisoning. [135] Neighbours violently quarrelled over a drain between their respective properties. [136] Disputes over rights of way and rights of water led to suits in which plaintiffs averred actual or potential breaches of the peace. [137] Forging of deeds and fraud were alleged. [138] Petty poaching and hunting offences, accompanied by exaggerated charges of assault, were made the business of the council. [139] Enclosures might lead to suits: allegations of wrongful or arbitrary enclosure of commons, and disputes about intake from the waste were the prominent charges. [140] Tithes were a related social problem. [141] A suit was initiated by a litigant who complained that his opponent had slandered him by reporting that he was openly perjured before Wolsey in another case; [142] and a captain of soldiers filed a bill alleging a slander by his subordinates while on service in Calais. [143] Of the suits filed concerning breach of

contract, one concerned the conditions for redeeming a
mortgage and two related to agreements and premiums for the
lease of land.[144] Matters in question between lords and their
tenants generally related to unpaid rents. Sometimes, however,
wider aspects of local jurisdiction would have to be settled by
the council.[145]

OFFICIAL PROSECUTIONS

Although litigation in star chamber between private parties
proliferated during the cardinal's ascendancy and afterwards,
official criminal prosecutions did not increase in the first half of
the sixteenth century. Only nine such cases are extant for
Wolsey's chancellorship. While this figure is undoubtedly a
minimum, the Ellesmere extracts, Hudson's notes and Hall's
Chronicle strongly suggest that these nine were the principal, if
not the only, instances.[146] In Henry VIII's reign, official
prosecutions rarely took place in star chamber; the council as a
rule confined itself to expediting such matters as were brought
to its attention by investigation and examination prior to
proceedings at common law.[147] The circumstances of the nine
prosecutions for which details survive indicate that such cases
under Wolsey were either connected with the council's
periodic demonstrations of law enforcement, or were promoted
by the cardinal for reasons of his own. The prosecutions were
meant to be exemplary. Five cases concerned offences against
public justice and public order, and were at the suit of the attorney-general. Two cases of *praemunire* were initiated. One
prosecution was for the wearing of a retainer's livery, and all
proceedings were *ore tenus*. The ninth case arose out of a
murder investigation.

Three of the attorney-general's suits concerned local corruption in Surrey. Inquiries were started in 1519 which brought to
light extensive rivalry between certain justices of the peace in
that county and revealed perversions of justice committed by
them since 1509.[148] Detailed investigations into judicial
misfeasance concentrated on maintenance and 'bearing'. Sir

Matthew Browne had maintained Henry Henley, John Scotte, John Russell and others at Guildford, and had procured an unlawful assembly which had 'overawed' sessions at Reigate.[149] Sir John A Legh and Lord Edmund Howard had maintained Thomas Powell against John Russell, Roger Legh against John Scotte, and William White against Sir Matthew Browne.[150] The result was the filing early in July 1519 of three written informations in star chamber, addressed by John Fitzjames, attorney-general, to Wolsey and the council. Each information began with a recitation of the circumstances: Fitzjames 'shewed' the council how 'the good rule and execucion of Justice in the Countie of Surrey hath been of long tyme lettyd and mysusyd by the grete mayntenance, enbrasery and berying' of the defendants, in public and private causes, 'to the grete hurte and damage of the kynges subjectes'. The informations then charged the three errant J.P.s with their specific offences.[151] The allegations against Browne included a charge of perjury. He had been ordered to make a true certificate to Wolsey and the council concerning the events in question, and 'being sworn to confess' his misdoings he had not confessed 'but cloaked the same'.

On 10 July, Browne foolishly denied the charges a second time before the council.[152] A Legh also denied his offences.[153] Lord Edmund Howard, more prudently in view of the thoroughness of the investigations, admitted his guilt in respect of five charges against him, and satisfactorily explained away the remaining two allegations.[154] In lieu of an answer, he filed a signed confession in which he besought Wolsey and the council 'to be mediators to the king's highness for hym . . . yn the premises'.[155] His case thereafter appears to have proceeded *ore tenus* and the final outcome was probably a pardon.[156] The cases of Browne and A Legh meanwhile continued, and the attorney-general filed replications to which rejoinders are not extant. Since rivalry had ensured the willingness of Browne to accuse A Legh and Howard and *vice versa*, and Howard had confessed, witnesses seem not to have been examined.

The cases came to final hearing on 28 October 1519. This

was also the day on which Sir William Bulmer submitted himself before the king and council after official proceedings *ore tenus* for wearing the duke of Buckingham's livery in the royal presence.[157] Henry VIII was sitting in person with forty of the council, and the timetable was arranged by Wolsey as a dramatic show of law enforcement: the previous day had been the occasion of the cardinal's second 'notable Oration' on the administration of justice.[158] It was five days before the speech that the chancellor had verbally alleged 'on the king's behalf' in star chamber that Bulmer had illegally become Buckingham's retainer and had dared to wear the duke's livery in the royal presence, despite the fact that he was already sworn as the king's servant.[159] Sir William confessed his offence and was committed to the Fleet until his appearance on 28 October; then, according to Wolsey's pre-arrangement, he submitted himself before the king and council. Predictably, Bulmer received a severe admonition from a furious Henry VIII; however, 'at the intercession of the Councell upon their knees', he was pardoned.[160] After Sir William had been taught 'a lesson to be Remembred', Browne and A Legh were led before the council. The hearing was quickly over: the defendants were fined £100 each and were to be committed to the Fleet.[161] Upon their 'submission and intercession', however, they too were pardoned.[162]

The fourth of the attorney-general's suits concerned a 'heinous' riot. In Henry VII's reign, temporary statutory provision had been made that where a riot was committed by forty or more persons, or was 'heinous', the record was to be sent to the king's council in order that appropriate action might be taken.[163] This procedure survived the expiry of the statute which created it, and continued in the reign of Henry VIII.[164] In 1525 such a riot was reported. The attorney-general, Ralph Swillington, filed an information in star chamber which alleged that John Devereux of Huntingdonshire and other rioters had forcibly intimidated the commissioners then attempting to collect the so-called 'amicable grant'. On 9 May Devereux and his co-defendants appeared before the council. After the information was read, they 'wholly submitted', and those who could write signed their confessions. Devereux was then committed to the Tower, and the other defendants were sent to the Fleet. [165] Ten days later, Devereux appeared again 'in his shirt', and upon his humble submission was discharged without fine and commanded to be 'of good abearing'. [166]

Of the fifth attorney-general's suit, nothing more is known than that on 11 February 1517 John Erneley was commanded 'to put in a bylle' against Edward Radley and other jurors of Abingdon, 'for perjurye by theym committed'. [167]

Both cases of *praemunire* were undertaken in 1518. The first was directed against Sir Christopher Plommer and Dr John Allen, and was a demonstration of Wolsey's power. The cardinal was in high favour with the king, [168] and he was successfully to exploit the coming of Lorenzo Campeggio to England as a final lever to force Leo X to grant him the long-coveted legatine commission *a latere*. [169] Dr Allen had been a protégé of Warham, though his precise offence is not known; [170] Plommer, the queen's chaplain, had been under investigation since October 1517, and was kept in London away from the court despite a protest from Queen Catherine to Wolsey. [171] Information had been laid before the council against the two clerics by the end of January 1518. [172] On 25 June they 'submitted them selves to the kinges mercye for theire offences concerninge the praemunire protestinge that they will noe further proceede in the defence of the said Cause'. [173] They were committed to the Fleet, and ordered to provide sureties for such fines as should be assessed by the council. The final decree was pronounced on 11 October following, and the defendants were fined a total of five hundred marks. [174] The fine was to be paid to the use of the king 'for the buyldyng, Reryng and finyshyng' of an extension to the *camera stellata*. For the payment of the fine, the defendants were bound by recognisance, each of them in a thousand marks, and so were dismissed 'from ony further apparaunce in this Courte at this tyme'. [175] Dr Allen subsequently became the cardinal's creature. His appointment as Wolsey's general commissary in 1519, at the beginning of the legate's attack on Warham's prerogative jurisdiction at Canterbury, no doubt added insult to injury in the eyes of the aged archbishop.[176]

The second case of *praemunire* was against Dr Henry Standish, who had been appointed bishop of St Asaph in 1518 despite Wolsey's support for a rival candidate.[177] Standish submitted in star chamber on 27 October of that year, confessing that he had received the rites of consecration from Warham before obtaining the royal assent and paying homage for his temporalities.[178] On 6 November following, he appeared a second time and exhibited a written confession which he read to the presence.[179] The case probably ended with a pardon. Dr Standish was one of the king's spiritual counsel, and he had been rescued by Henry VIII three years previously from the wrath of convocation during the controversial sequel to the Hunne affair.[180] At the height of the crisis of 1515, and at Standish's citation before the assembly at the Blackfriars, the judges had declared that the entire clergy in convocation were liable to the penalties of *praemunire*.[181] Wolsey, subsequently at Baynard's castle, had been obliged to kneel before the king and make a partial submission, urging that the clergy had no thought of diminishing the royal prerogative. Standish owed his bishopric to Henry's patronage. It was richly ironic that Wolsey so successfully secured the new bishop's humiliation for offences 'in derogacion of the kinge and of his prerogative Royall'.[182] The cardinal always possessed an adroit facility for paying off old scores.

The remaining official prosecution also took place mainly in 1518. In the course of a murder investigation by the council, the two principal suspects made a full confession which implicated Sir Robert Sheffield, a former recorder of London and a councillor. As a result, Sheffield was charged with being an accessary to felony.[183] There were, however, sinister political overtones. Sheffield had been speaker of Henry VIII's anticlerical second parliament, which had sessions in 1512 and 1514, and he had in 1515 joined as a leader of the deputation to the king which resulted in the dramatic debate at the Blackfriars.[184] In late 1516 he was sent to the Tower and fined the sum of eight thousand marks by Wolsey for 'opprobrious words' concerning these events. [185] By July 1517 he had again been committed to the Tower 'for contempts'. [186] On 6 February 1518, Sheffield appeared in star chamber on the new charges, and it was clear that a dangerous situation was at hand. Wolsey himself conducted the examination of the accused, and Sheffield acknowledged himself to be an accessary to murder according to the confession of the original suspects. [187] But the cardinal also resurrected the past. Sheffield was obliged to submit again for his 'unfitting words' of 1516, and was compelled to affirm that he came to his stupendous fine of that year only through the 'charitable' mediation of Wolsey. Sir Robert was also required to confess more recent words that the cardinal 'advanced this cause against him of malice'. [188] He was then committed a third time to the Tower, to be kept there 'as a felon and accessorie to ample precedent for such precaution. The practice of the murther'. [189] In addition, Sheffield was given four days to answer whether he would 'at his jeopardy and adventure' rely on a pardon he had obtained as a justice of the peace in 1516; [190] Sir Robert had given notice of his intention to plead the pardon against his part in the murder. However, 'divers doubts' had rightly been expressed by the judges as to whether a pardon could be effective against an offence not envisaged when it was granted; in any case, Sir Robert's involvement had persisted beyond the granting of the pardon. [191]

On the following Wednesday, Wolsey conducted a more abrasive examination. Further details concerning the handling of the murdered man had come to light and Sheffield again confessed, admitting in the process that he had committed perjury in his previous examination. The questioning then reverted to further 'opprobrious words' alleged to have been spoken by Sir Robert with reference to the crisis of 1515. 'Alsoo wher he saied that it was unhappy that the lordes temporall warr at variaunce at that tyme, for hadd not that been my lorde Cardinales hedd shulde have been as Red as his cote was, he saieth that he rememberth not that he spake the same woordes'. [192] The examination ended with Wolsey demanding Sheffield's 'determinate answer' whether he intended to rely on his pardon, and three more days were granted for the accused to debate the point with his counsel. On the following Saturday, Sheffield made his last appearance in star chamber.[193] First he confessed that he had spoken the offending words concerning the variance between the lords temporal, for which he begged forgiveness. Then, on the question of the pardon, he put himself 'hooly in the kinges grace and mercie': mounting the council board at Wolsey's direction and there kneeling before all the council, he 'did not aloonly surrendre his patent of his pardon . . . but alsoo with his owen handes did cutte and Cancell the same', and at Wolsey's further command 'did breke the seale of the same pardon in peces'.[194] Sir Robert Sheffield had endured the fullest rigour of the cardinal's court. He was returned to the Tower, and died there seven months later.[195]

4

Private Litigation

PLEADINGS AND PROOFS

Litigation in suits between party and party began with the bill of complaint. The bill was a written declaration in English, which explained the plaintiff's grief and the supposed wrong done by the defendant, requested remedy, and prayed for the issue of process in order that the alleged offender might be compelled to appear before the lords of the council to answer concerning the premisses.[1] Pleas for redress in star chamber were nearly always in general terms, unlike chancery where the plaintiff urged some specific remedy available there.[2] Bills of complaint were drawn with the advice of counsel, first roughly on paper and then on parchment in a formal engrossing-hand, after which they were presented to the clerk of the council for filing. In star chamber, bills were correctly addressed to the sovereign, although in practice many early Tudor bills were directed to the lord chancellor as in chancery.[3] Most documents were professionally prepared, although a number were drawn by the plaintiffs themselves. Throughout its development, the English bill retained the format of the petition. The tone was that of supplication on the part of the 'loyal subject' and 'humble orator', and daily

prayers for the health, longevity and prosperous estate of the
sovereign were proffered beside the charges against the defendant. In the fifteenth century, bills had been short and contained only the bare minimum of information; later, however,
increasing circumstantial detail was included which could
prove more than sufficient to enable the defendant to answer
and the court to proceed.

The material content of the bill of complaint was supposed
to be true and to be set down plainly and certainly.[4] In reality,
although the subject-matter of star chamber bills varied with
the suit, the most common ingredient was the almost in-
variable recital of riot, forcible entry or trespass. The real subject of the complaint often remained directly unspecified,
although it might not be difficult to diagnose. When William
and Joan Nype of Coventry reported how Thomas Banewell
'with dyverse other Ryoters and evyll dysposyd persons to the
nombre of iij or iiij to your said Oratours unknowen' had forcibly prevented them from taking possession of a freehold estate which they claimed by inheritance, the probability was
that their right and title to the property was a good deal less
clear than they alleged, and that this uncertainty rather than
the 'riot' lay behind their suit.[5] As an alternative pleading to
the bill of complaint, a written information by a private individual might initiate litigation. In theory, the distinction
between the bill and the information was that the bill was appropriate when a private individual was himself the aggrieved
party, and the information when some wrong done to the
crown was alleged. Such informations usually described
themselves as 'for the king's advantage' and were adopted in
cases of officers' malfeasance or intrusions on the king's
possession.[6] In practice, however, the distinction was not
rigidly maintained, and individuals exhibited informations on
purely private matters which were acceptable to the council.[7]

The cardinal's court knew no satisfactory procedure for the
supervision and scrutiny of bills of complaint with a view to the
summary dismissal of frivolous suits, despite the existence of
ample precedent for such precaution. The practice of the
fifteenth century, confirmed by parliament, was that the courts

of equitable proceedings required plaintiffs to produce sureties
for the payment of damages to their opponents should the
latter be unjustly vexed, 'for avoiding of causelesse and trifling
suites, to which most men be overprone'.[8] In Henry VII's
reign, prospective plaintiffs in star chamber were bound in
their own and in other sureties to prove their complaints or to
pay the costs of defendants.[9] In the early years of Henry VIII's
reign, when Warham remained in office as chancellor, this
practice was continued;[10] but under Wolsey sureties were not
generally required, although a number of plaintiffs voluntarily offered to satisfy the defendants' expenses should
the allegations in their bills prove to be unfounded.[11] The
cardinal, at least initially, seems not to have considered unnecessary litigation to be a problem. In their enthusiasm to
assist plaintiffs, lord chancellors could show an inconsiderate
ignorance of the interests of defendants. Wolsey did not insist
that bills should be signed by counsel, although this safeguard
was to be required in star chamber after May 1549 as in
chancery;[12] he did not require plaintiffs to swear to the truth of
their bills before process issued.[13] On the contrary, the point of
development was reached where conciliar process returnable
in star chamber issued as a matter of course, with the exception of notorious cases, and then only because special orders
were made prescribing high penalties in default of appearance
by defendants. Moreover, Wolsey regularly allowed the issue
of process before the bill of complaint was filed, a procedural
abuse which meant that the plaintiff need not have finalised
nor in any way committed himself to an accusation until his
opponent's arrival in London.[14] In chancery also the ancient
policy of examining bills before the issue of process was allowed to lapse. The cardinal was inevitably accused of selling
writs of *subpoena* for money.[15] He was, however, not alone:
despite the concern of Sir Thomas More, Sir Thomas
Wriothesley and Sir Richard Rich, who variously aimed to
revert to more stringent practices in chancery and star
chamber, the other sixteenth-century chancellors prior to Sir
Nicholas Bacon were less severe, preferring to extend the
development and organisation of their courts rather than to

restrict the availability of facilities for litigation. [16]

If the plaintiff had filed the bill of complaint at the time of suing out of process, he would be allowed to amend his bill or to substitute a new one up to the day scheduled for the return of process. But amendment was not possible after the defendant had entered his appearance. If process had been issued first, the plaintiff had to perfect and exhibit a bill by the time of the defendant's appearance. Should he fail in this, the defendant could secure his dismissal with expenses for his wrongful vexation. [17] In the absence of a bill, the defendant or his counsel moved the court for a dismissal with costs, which would be granted by an order. Motions of this sort were all too frequent by the time of Wolsey's last year in office: on 12 June 1529 the cardinal therefore pronounced a general order which established that if the bill of complaint was not ready by the day following the defendant's appearance, the latter was to be dismissed automatically with costs, and the costs were to be taxed by the clerk of the council in the absence of the chancellor. [18]

The original process of the council was the writ *quibusdam certis de causis* which had been devised in the chancery about the year 1346. [19] The writ commanded appearance *coram consilio nostro* under penalty but, as its title implied, did not specify the precise cause of summons. Although first issued under the great seal, the writ was almost immediately translated into French and issued under the privy seal, being designated as *le brief sur certeine peine*. [20] By the reign of Henry VI, the instrument was the established procedural usage of the council and was translated into English. [21] In Henry VII's time, it generally issued in a standard form apart from the amount of the penalty which varied from £40 to £100. [22] Robert Midwinter's summons, dated 22 January 1491, required him 'for certain causes and consideracions us and our Counsaill moeving' to 'personally appere afor us and our said Counsaill' upon pain of £100. [23] Midwinter arrived at the palace of Westminster four and a half weeks later, and Robert Rydon, clerk of the council in star chamber, recorded his due appearance by an endorsement on the returned writ, admitting him as a defendant '*coram consilio domini Regis'*.[24] The privy seal summons continued in frequent use to effect appearances in star chamber well into the reign of Henry VIII, the penalty varying from £100 to £500,[25] and an isolated instance of the method might occur as late as the 1550s.[26] The form of process which became preferred in star chamber under Wolsey was, however, the writ of *subpoena*.[27] The *subpoena* was the earliest Latin form of the *quibusdam certis de causis* with the *sub pena* clause inserted; the writ issued out of chancery under the great seal and was returnable in star chamber, where it was correctly described as the *subpoena ad comparendum*.[28] The penalty for default of appearance was usually £100, but rose to £200 or more by order of the chancellor in notorious cases of delinquency.[29] By the end of the reign of Henry VIII, the great seal process had secured an exclusive position in star chamber.[30] Prior to the 1530s, however, this had not become settled and several plaintiffs requested privy seal summonses or writs of *subpoena* in the alternative.[31]

Process summoned defendants to appear in person on a fixed day of return, which would be from four to twelve weeks after the issue of the writ, depending on the distance in time between the date of issue and the next suitable return day. The council in star chamber organised its judicial business according to the law terms and the return days were those set for the common law courts. In serious cases of misdemeanour, the defendant might be instructed to appear immediately on receipt of the writ or within a week, or on pain of allegiance, but these instances were exceptional.[32] The normal rule was that defendants were to appear in star chamber on or before a specified return day under penalty of £100. The £100 was not enforceable in default of appearance, being *in terrorem tantum*. However, if the defendant disobeyed the summons, he would on his subsequent appearance, by due process of contempt, be bound in a recognisance to his future appearance. Should he fail to keep this, the penalty of the recognisance would be forfeit to the crown and leviable.[33]

Service of process was left to the plaintiff or his agent. The duty was neither easy nor safe. Richard Clark, attempting to serve a privy seal in 1516, was obliged 'to abide still in a Parlor where he delivered it, and to drinke whether he would or not'.[34] To avoid insult and intimidation, most attempts at service of process were made in church, or the writ was left at the defendant's house where it was frequently nailed to the door.[35] It was sometimes possible to hire a process-server privately, and the sheriff of the county might act for a fee.[36] The services of a sergeant-at-arms might be engaged, but probably only if the defendant was in London or by order of the council.[37] If there was more than usual difficulty in effecting a valid service or if the defendant failed to appear, the plaintiff or his process-server and any available witnesses might be examined in open court by the council on the details of the service.[38] On 10 November 1525, Michael Thomas deposed that on the Sunday after Hallowe'en at St Elwys in Cornwall he attempted to serve a writ of *subpoena* on William Tallack, who refused to receive it. Thomas finally laid it on the ground near Tallack, but the latter refused to pick it up.[39] Alternatively sworn affidavits would be taken out of court by the clerk of the council for subsequent use.[40] By the cardinal's general order of 21 May 1527, the clerk was authorised not merely to take these affidavits but also to act on them, initiating process of contempt without further order.[41] More than one deposition or affidavit was preferred; the plaintiff's word alone might, however, be accepted.[42] When sufficient evidence of a valid service had been received, the defendant – failing his belated appearance – immediately became vulnerable to process of contempt.

Privy seal summonses and writs of *subpoena* were reasonably effective in securing appearances. The instrument employed in the face of disobedience by defendants was the writ of attachment, which required the sheriff of the county to produce the delinquent at the next return day to answer for his contempt as well as to the matter preferred against him before the council.[43] Further lack of success was met by attachment with proclamation, and finally a commission of rebellion.[44] The first two stages of the procedure are documented in the case of the Mexborne family.[45] In 1523 Robert Benger was awarded five separate writs of *subpoena* against the Mexbornes. They failed to appear and Benger was examined on oath as to the validity of the services. After examination, the council ordered that a writ of attachment should be directed to the sheriff of Yorkshire to effect the appearance of the defendants. The sheriff, however, returned '*non sunt inventi*', and in consequence a writ of attachment with proclamation was addressed to him containing a penalty clause of £300.[46] Whether this produced a better result is unknown; if not, a commission of rebellion would have ensued, addressed to such commissioners as were named by the plaintiff and approved by the council. If it was reported to the council that a sheriff had failed to execute a writ of attachment and simply returned '*non est inventus*', an attachment with proclamation would immediately issue and the sheriff would himself be served with a *subpoena* returnable in star chamber.[47] After proof of his negligence, an offending sheriff would be imprisoned in the Fleet.[48] Early in Henry VIII's reign, process of attachment might be preceded by a writ of *subpoena* or privy seal charging the defendant to his allegiance.[49] After the general order of 1527, however, standardised process of contempt issued as the course of the court, beginning with attachment upon examination or affidavit made concerning the alleged disobedience. If all efforts to command the appearance of the defendant failed, the council might proceed in a case for title of land to grant an injunction to the plaintiff for possession until the defendant had appeared, answered and purged his contempt.[50]

When the defendant presented his person in star chamber, the clerk of the council would make the entry of the appearance. The defendant was then 'admitted' into court and was obliged to exhibit his answer to the plaintiff's bill of complaint. When the answer was presented, the defendant would be sworn as to the truth of his statement. Defendants who delayed would be commanded by the council to answer and be sworn.[51] Answers were drawn with the advice of counsel and were engrossed on parchment. They began with words of art: the bill of complaint was 'insufficient in law to be answered unto' and designed to put the defendant to unnecessary vexation and costs. The matter complained of was stated invariably to be 'untrue', 'uncertain' and 'determinable by the course of the common law and not in this honourable court'. The last was not considered to be a serious legal plea unless specific argument was advanced. After these formal beginnings, the majority of defendants proceeded to answer the facts and declare the truth as they perceived it. Answers then concluded with a further repetition of the inaccuracies of the bill of complaint, a prayer for dismissal with expenses, and confident assertions by defendants of their willingness to prove their case to the satisfaction of the council. In Henry VII's reign and early in Henry VIII's, some defendants answered by simply entering a plea of not guilty.[52] By the 1520s, however, answers – in company with all the written pleadings – had begun to grow in length and complexity.

Unless the claim that a case was properly determinable at law be regarded as a plea to the council's jurisdiction, which in practice it was not, the demurrer in lieu of answer does not number amongst the pleadings of the early Tudor period. Nevertheless, a few litigants attempted to combine a challenge to the jurisdiction of the court with an answer. When freehold title was in dispute, a defendant might advance a plea against determination by extra-legal process, while at the same time recognising star chamber's right to punish any alleged riots.[53] No doubt he hoped to secure dismissal with costs by coming to issue on an alleged but probably fictitious riot only. And in cases which included charges of assault and battery resulting in premature death, the defendant might claim (before going on to answer) that the bill was only determinable 'by the Course of the commen lawe and not elles where, for asmoche as it touchith mannys liff'.[54] These pleas were not accepted. Star chamber remained hostile to demurrers, 'for that it is an offence to the Jurisdiccion of the Courte to demurre, and Costes putt uppon him that doth demurre, yf it be ruled against him'.[55]

Answer was exhibited on oath. Contrary to the practice in chancery, the defendant was then examined on any questions of fact arising. In Henry VII's reign there was only one stage:

defendants, having been sworn, went on to make a short
declaration.[56] This statement was endorsed on the answer by
the clerk of the council, although if it was long a separate sheet
of paper was used.[57] The procedure was at an elementary
stage. Under the cardinal, a more developed form for the examination of defendants may be detected. There might be two
stages. The defendant first swore that his answer was true.
Then, if the plaintiff had filed written interrogatories for use in
the examination, the questions he had devised were put to the
defendant on oath, and the answers given were written down
in a paper book by the clerk. On 26 January 1529, John Jenny
was sworn first upon his answer and then on the plaintiff's
interrogatories.[58] Two days later, William Huntley was sworn
on his answer and then upon interrogatories. The examination
was evidently substantial, since it was continued the next
day.[59] Some defendants were examined in considerable detail
and more than once.[60] The cardinal himself might intervene
and conduct an examination of a defendant in a case of
misdemeanour.[61] The procedure followed would vary in
length in each case, and the council retained its discretionary
powers to examine defendants as was necessary. Increasingly,
however, plaintiffs dictated the format of defendants' examinations by the submission in advance of written interrogatories, and only once was the method questioned.[62] If,
after examination, the council was persuaded that a defendant
was the victim of a frivolous suit and that *prima facie* the case
against him could not be proven, he would be discharged with
costs.[63] However, such dismissals were not often possible and
the council had to be on constant guard against perjury.
Should perjury be discovered in the examination, the defendant would be punished by being compelled to wear
humiliating papers in Westminster hall or by imprisonment in
the Fleet.[64] Under Wolsey, the council in star chamber
punished perjury whenever it was detected, whether or not it
was complained of by bill.[65]

Since the defendant was required to swear to the truth of his
answer and undergo examination, he had to appear in person.
If for an acceptable reason he could not make a personal

appearance, the council, after sworn affidavit by his representative, would commission gentlemen of credit in the locality
where the defendant resided to receive the answer under
authority of a writ of *dedimus potestatem.*[66] Early in Henry VIII's
reign, these affidavits of indisposition were taken in open
court;[67] by the end of Wolsey's chancellorship, however, the
clerk of the council took them out of court.[68] Acceptable
reasons for the purpose of a commission were danger to life
resulting from travel to London, extreme age or ill health. Full
details of the infirmities of defendants were advanced in
affidavits: octagenarians could not appear 'without danger of
their persons' being 'so sick and diseased'.[69] A septuagenarian
suffered severe pain from 'a sore leg' and could not ride.[70]
Others were 'diseased and impotent' or 'sick of the ague', and
one sorry defendant 'hath a greate wenn in his necke running
sometymes Corrupt matter and blood in such quantity that the
beholders marvaile hee bleedeth not to death'.[71] The
commission *ad recipiendum responsionem* would be attached to the
bill of complaint itself or to a copy. By its authority, the commissioners were to take the defendant's answer, swear him to
the truth of his statement and examine him on the subject-
matter of the bill, making certificate in writing under seal of
their proceedings by a stated day of return in the following
term.[72] In the reign of Henry VII, it had been usual to extend
the terms of commissions *ad recipiendum responsionem* to include
also the commission *ad examinandum testes*, by virtue of which
the examination of witnesses as well as defendants might be
effected in the locality.[73] This would further aid the
defendant's conduct of his case, while hopefully speeding the
suit and avoiding expense to both parties. The expedient continued under Wolsey. Later, however, the two elements were
subject to separate writs of authority.[74]

When the defendant personally appeared in star chamber to
file his answer and was sworn and examined, he might be admitted to attorney and licensed to depart or, depending on the
nature of the case and the council's discretion, required to
make future appearances in person. Prior to Wolsey's
supremacy, admissions to attorney were not a matter of

course. A special order was required to discharge each defendant from personal attendance.[75] Cases in star chamber were at first sight criminal or quasi-criminal, and in consequence defendants would be enjoined to make themselves available and not to depart without licence.[76] Eventually increasing business made it necessary to recognise the true situation. The majority of suits were in fact essentially civil in character. On 5 February 1527, the cardinal decided that those defendants accused of riot who did not confess any riot in their answers should be admitted to attorney and licensed to depart.[77] Later the same year, in Wolsey's general order of 21 May, the ruling was confirmed. The clerk of the council was to effect admissions to attorney without further reference to the lord chancellor.[78] The development was unquestionably necessary in purely civil litigation. In criminal suits, however, and in cases where the defendant had offered disobedience or contempt, the conditions of personal appearance remained as they had been in the reign of Henry VII. The daily attendance of the defendant throughout the term might be required, and Wolsey regarded this expensive inconvenience to the defendant as suitable chastisement in notorious cases. Sir William Brereton complained that he had made his appearance from day to day for almost a year.[79] But he was co-defendant in an unpleasant case of local corruption and violent death, and if nothing else his presence in London enabled evidence to be collected against him in Cheshire by commissioners acting under a writ of *dedimus potestatem* without his undue interference.[80] In these instances, the defendant was ordered to enter into a recognisance for his daily appearance in sums varying from £50 to £1000.[81] Additional sureties might also be required, who were obliged to enter into recognisances of £40 to 1000 marks.[82] Defendants would be required to appear before the council from day to day, on specified days of return or upon 'resonable warnyng and monicion';[83] they could be commanded not to depart beyond a radius of ten miles from the city of London without the licence of the lord chancellor.[84] Those suspected of misdemeanour would also be bound to keep the peace and to be 'of good abearing'.[85] The system was flexible, so much so that the cardinal harnessed it to keeping order in his own household: on 7 October 1526, Thomas Strangways, Wolsey's controller, was bound by recognisance in £1000 not to molest Thomas Cromwell and his servants, the latter having been threatened with 'bodily hurt'.[86] Alternatively a defendant in star chamber might be required to pay to the clerk of the council a sum required as security for the peace in cash or plate.[87] Defendants in misdemeanour would be committed to the Fleet after answer and examination pending completion of the formalities of recognisance. When they and their sureties were bound, they would be discharged from that already overcrowded institution.[88] Those who subsequently failed in their appearances or behaviour would be promptly recommitted to prison for contempt, and their recognisances would be deemed forfeit and leviable.[89]

The second stage in the exchange of written pleadings was that of replication and rejoinder. These documents, like bill and answer, were drawn with the advice of counsel and engrossed on parchment. The replication was the plaintiff's response to the defendant's answer; it affirmed and developed the bill, and denied or traversed the defendant's argument.[90] A few replications consisted of a detailed refutation of the answer, introducing new fact and circumstance in support of the plaintiff's case or simply repeating the full facts as stated in the bill of complaint. Usually, however, a short denial of the defendant's answer was employed, and the plaintiff maintained his previous arguments in general terms. A well-drawn replication could do much to shore up a suit, although the plaintiff could not alter his basic case from that as exhibited in the bill of complaint. The defendant's rejoinder was designed to counteract the plaintiff's replication. It affirmed the truth of the answer, and might traverse each material part of the replication.[91] Few rejoinders were in fact substantial, and most were short, crisp and formal. Very rarely, the plaintiff continued the argument by exhibiting a surrejoinder to challenge the factual content of the defendant's rejoinder.[92] Replication and rejoinder were the normal procedure in star chamber; but in the minority of cases where the defendant had answered the bill of complaint with a simple plea of not guilty, replication and rejoinder would be omitted. The plea of not guilty put the plaintiff's case in issue and no further pleadings were possible.[93] Where a replication was required, however, and the plaintiff failed to file one, the defendant might secure his dismissal with costs by motion before the council.[94]

After the exchange of written pleadings, the parties were at issue and the examination of witnesses could begin. In the reign of Henry VII, the procedure for examinations was at a stage of incipient development. The parties produced their witnesses and sometimes provided interrogatories for their examination. The questioning was managed by an examiner, either a councillor or the clerk of the council, and the depositions were recorded on paper in a continuous narrative. All was done in open court.[95] The origins of these arrangements may be traced from the time when the king's council, after receiving a petition, might conduct the entire case *viva voce*. During Wolsey's supremacy, star chamber's mature procedure emerged, and by the cardinal's fall it had become settled in its important aspects.

Examination of witnesses in London usually began after the defendant had rejoined, but witnesses might be produced by either party after the defendant had himself been sworn and examined.[96] This convenience assisted both the litigants and the council. A day would be given to the party to produce his witnesses for questioning.[97] The witnesses appeared by arrangement with their sponsor, who guaranteed their expenses, and no doubt they arrived in most cases suitably charged as to the evidence they should give. If a necessary witness refused to attend, upon sworn examination of the party concerned as to the circumstances, a privy seal summons or writ of *subpoena ad testificandum* would be issued against the reluctant deponent. On 10 July 1525, Sir Thomas Tyrrell affirmed that William Garsington was 'necessary' to his case and that he had 'offred hym his reasonable costes to come upp and depose . . . which he refused to doo'.[98] A writ of *subpoena* was accordingly awarded against Garsington. Examinations in the early years of the reign of Henry VIII were still taken in open court. However, by the end of the cardinal's rule they could be taken out of court, a councillor or a committee of councillors, the clerk or one of the assistant clerks, acting as examiner.[99] If councillors were officiating as examiners, a clerk acted as secretary. Interrogatories to be put to the witnesses were supplied ready drawn on paper by the party, having been drafted in consultation with counsel. The number of questions varied: in the 1520s between five and ten questions were usual. By the 1530s, interrogatories might include forty or more items. The questions covered the ground of the written pleadings point by point, and it is notable that inquiries as to the fictitious riots and notional violence included in bills of complaint were often to be found in opening interrogatories *ex parte* the plaintiff. Witnesses were undoubtedly susceptible to subornation.

After each witness was produced, the day on which he was sworn and for which party he appeared were noted by the clerk at the head of the paper on which the depositions were to be taken. The witness then gave his name, age, profession and usually his dwelling place. He then answered each interrogatory in turn, as tendered by the examiner. Richard Ebbis, examined on 4 December 1528 *ex parte* lady Catherine Willoughby, deposed first that he had no advance knowledge that Sir Christopher Willoughby intended to make a forcible entry (probably genuine) into the lordship of Eresby in Lincolnshire the preceding February.[100] To the second interrogatory, he said that six persons accompanied Sir Christopher with 'swerdes and buklers'. Thirdly, the entry was forcible since, although 'ther was noo bodye to make ony resistance . . . within the said Lordshipp', Sir Christopher required his 'horsekeaper' to 'clyme over the gate . . . and when he was over, brake the lokke of the same gate'. Other factual and circumstantial questioning followed. Lastly, Ebbis deposed how Sir Christopher, wishing to gain entry to the 'evidence hous' but being counselled not to do so forcibly by his man of law, 'commaunded one Thomas à Carvar . . . to take frome under the doore of the said hous two great Sande stones; which amoved . . . caused the said Thomas to crepe under the doore, who so did and ... opened the lock on the inside'. The statements of witnesses were formally set out by the clerk of the council, preserving the phraseology of the questions. If a deponent did not know the answer to an item, it was entered 'that he can make no answer'. After the last question had been answered, the witness read through his depositions and signed them. If he could not write, his mark was witnessed by the clerk. When each witness presented by a party had been examined, the sheets of depositions would be made into a book, and the interrogatories would be attached to the first page with a pin.

Examinations were conducted in private, and the depositions were kept secret until the council ordered publication. Depositions taken after publication would be declared invalid.[101] Both sides had separate examinations, and a witness might not be examined more than once on each side. Witnesses could, however, be cross-examined by either side. There may have been a good deal of tactical manoeuvre involved in early Tudor examinations, for there is no evidence in these years of any orders or measures to prevent the concealment of strategic witnesses and the abuse of cross-examinations. In Elizabeth's reign, by general order of the court, every principal witness produced by either party had to be shown to the attorney for the other side, and the names of lesser witnesses were to be written on paper and handed over. Names and dwelling places were to be revealed, and this was to be done either before any witnesses were examined, or before the departure of witnesses from the presence of the examiner. If the other side put in cross-interrogatories against any witness, he was to be examined on them before his departure from London, and if he refused under the encouragement of his sponsor, a writ of attachment was obtainable against him.[102] Such precautions were not taken under Wolsey.

In the early Tudor star chamber, most examining of witnesses was done at the centre. The parties might, however, procure the issue of a commission *ad examinandum testes*, which would be addressed to persons of good credit in the country by writ of *dedimus potestatem*.[103] After the defendant had rejoined, the opportunity to join in commission for the taking of proofs was available to litigants by consent of the parties and the council without limitation to instances of ill health and indisposition.[104] When the parties decided on a commission and the commissioners had been named, the clerk of the council prepared the warrant for the writ of *dedimus potestatem*. When the writ issued, it was attached to a copy of the pleadings previously exhibited by the respective parties.[105] Interrogatories might also be supplied for the use of the commissioners. The writ instructed the commissioners to swear the witnesses, examine them and record their statements. The depositions were to be engrossed on parchment and returned into star chamber under seal by a fixed day of return.[106]

After the completion of the examination of witnesses, 'publication' ensued by which the depositions were placed on the public file and the parties and their attorneys were permitted to take copies in order that each side might prepare its case.[107] A motion for final hearing was then made, by party or attorney, and a day was set by the council for determination.[108] In theory, cases might come to hearing in two ways: after the exchange of written pleadings and the taking of proofs as described, or after sworn confession made by a defendant in his examination. In practice, however, only three definite examples of the latter method occurred under Wolsey in suits between party and party.[109] If a party was out of town, his attorney had the duty of informing him when publication had passed and the day for the hearing had been settled.[110]

DETERMINATION

The hearing of suits at the centre was either in open court before the council or it might be before an *ad hoc* committee of councillors specially appointed to reduce the outstanding work. Counsel for the plaintiff recited the content of the bill of complaint and counsel for the defendant replied with the substance of the answer. Any facts which had emerged in later pleadings were stated, and extracts from the depositions of the

witnesses and any other relevant documents, especially deeds
of title, were read or produced for inspection.[111] The council
then debated the points at issue. If, after 'deliberation' and the
'advice' of the judges and sergeants-at-law, there was clear un-
animity of opinion, the lord chancellor would pronounce judgment in the form of a decree. But in civil cases this rarely
happened. It may be that the cardinal's conciliar committees
had time to hear and determine more cases than the few for
which evidence is extant.[112] As far as its plenary sessions were
concerned, however, the council relied heavily on reference, arbitration and compromise. In criminal cases, judgment might
come more swiftly. The cardinal made his decision on the
facts, and it did not take long to commit the defendant to the
Fleet or to order fine, pillory or wearing of papers.[113] On 13
July 1518, a case of extortion was heard against John
Vesacreley. Wolsey found the offence proved and decreed that
the defendant 'shalbe immediatlye convayed to the Fleete' until the next day 'at Markett tyme', when he was to be 'sett uppon the Pillorye with a large paper uppon his head, wherein
shalbe wrytten in greate lettres "this man hathe committed ex-
torcion" '. The defendant was then to be returned to prison
until he had repaid four marks to the plaintiff.[114]

The majority of suits, however, were primarily civil in content and concerned an unquiet title. Even those cases in which
the violence alleged by plaintiffs was more than simply
notional turned upon the respective titles of the parties, though
'riot' might be separately found and punished. What appears
most often to have happened was that the chancellor, after
publication, either referred the question of title to the judges,
or invoked arbitration or compromise. At this point, the plaintiff would be well advised to move the chancellor to grant an
injunction for possession in his favour pending further
outcome.[115] He thus left the initiative with the defendant. If
the latter perceived that he had the weaker case and was
prepared to cut his losses, the suit would surcease without
further proceedings. The plaintiff's object was, after all, to
secure satisfaction not to win a lawsuit. But defendants never
seem to have given up hope. For this reason dismissal of suits

to the common law after an initial hearing was not a satisfactory expedient, although it was sometimes tried by the council in the cases of suspected time-wasters or where the parties were obstinate and refused to consider arbitration or compromise. Suits merely turned up again after brief intervals. The dispute between the Savage and Aston families and the Dutton family survived an attempted dismissal to law in 1528, resuming in star chamber two years later when Sir Thomas More referred it to the judges.[116] Reference of the title to expert legal opinion or committal of the case to independent persons of repute for settlement were therefore the usual procedures followed by the council.

The decision as to which course of action should be applied was the lord chancellor's. He would take into account the circumstances of a suit, the desires of the parties, their sincerity and willingness to settle their differences, and the requirement that the council should be the means to the achievement of solutions which were fair and in accordance with the principles of equitable proceedings. Reference of the 'title in variance' to two of the senior judges would be ordered if legal learning was needed to clarify a complex case, or if determination in a stricter legal sense was required. This was a procedure already established in the reign of Henry VII which was continued and developed under Henry VIII,[117] being especially favoured by Sir Thomas More when in office.[118] Titles to land or goods would be referred for examination and report;[119] the parties and their advisers presented their evidence before the judges appointed to hear their arguments and peruse their documents, after which a considered legal opinion would be sent to the chancellor. Judges named by Wolsey for the purpose included Sir Robert Brudenell, Sir Richard Broke, Sir Humphrey Coningsby, Richard Elyot, Sir John Fitzjames and John More.[120] The formalities of reference usually took about six months. Then, when the report of the judges had been received, it was made the basis of the council's decision, being incorporated into a final decree for possession and execution. On 10 July 1525, Wolsey had referred the unquiet title to the manor of Maidwell, Northamptonshire, disputed between

John Haselwood and Thomas Seyton, to Sir Robert Brudenell and Sir John Fitzjames.[121] After scrutiny, the judges discovered that the manor had been the subject of 'an indenture of award' between the present parties and certain other persons in February 1516, subsequent to a previously agreed settlement by arbitration. When this information had been received in star chamber, Wolsey and the council decreed – on 1 February 1526 – that the earlier award 'be kept and performed in every behalfe'.[122] Thus, since Haselwood was sole successor in title to the interest which had prevailed in respect of Maidwell in 1516, the cardinal pronounced that 'the same John Haselwode and his heyres shall from hensforth peasably hold and enjoye the seid manor of Maydwell . . . without lett or disturbance of the seid Thomas Seyton or his heyres or assignes'.

More frequently, however, the cardinal decided on the second course of action. Arbitration and compromise in private suits were at a premium in all the council courts, not least for historical reasons. Mediation was of the essence of conciliar jurisdiction: in civil suits before the medieval king's council, parties would voluntarily submit *in alto et basso,* agreeing to abide by its decision.[123] The appeal to mediators was in practice the only viable way to effect settlements, especially in cases where some right lay on both sides. The procedures of mediation were versatile and applicable to all categories of civil litigation. Lastly, the system did not exclude those unlearned in the law – notably the cardinal – from active intervention. By appointing himself as the principal mediator in star chamber, Wolsey could indeed satisfy his ambition to draw *causes célèbres* unto himself, thereby obliging litigants to take advantage of his brilliant intellect and ideas of natural justice.

In practical terms, arbitration and compromise were far from being mutually exclusive: a compromise solution, arrived at by commissioners and accepted by the parties, might be couched as an 'award' or 'arbitrament'. There were, however, basic differences. Sir Thomas More observed to Peter Giles how his time was fully occupied with legal matters, 'at one moment pleading or hearing, at another giving an award as arbiter or deciding a case as umpire'. [124] The contrast is between common law and conciliar proceedings – but, within the latter half of the device, arbitration and 'umpiring' are surely distinct alternatives? This had been so in the fifteenth century: the dispute between the bishop and the dean and chapter of Exeter, and the mayor and citizens, had long 'honged yn debate' before the council when in August 1447 the parties were bound to 'come to an arbitrament'. The lord chancellor and the two chief justices were appointed arbitrators. Nevertheless, pending the award, influences were at work attempting to persuade the parties to settle the matter by 'entreaty' at home. [125] There were, in particular, doctrinal differences. An 'arbitrament' had to offer a degree of satisfaction to both sides, the parties were required to have valid legal claims to what was awarded to them, and a settlement by indenture of award would be deemed enforceable by common law judges. [126] Compromise was wholly extra-legal and, although a settlement might be enforced in a conciliar court, it did not prejudice future litigation at law. Common to both approaches, however, was the principle of mutual consent: settlements could not be imposed upon unwilling parties.

Prior to Wolsey, arbitration had generally comprised the mediation of the lord chancellor and legal personnel acting in an extra-judicial fashion. [127] The cardinal continued to employ the lawyers in this capacity but also introduced others into the field, notably councillors, the civilians of the chancery and the members of Wolsey's own household. [128] When suits were to be sent to arbitration, the parties were bound by recognisances in varying amounts which obliged them to attend upon the arbitrators in person when required, to observe such award as might eventually be indented, and sometimes to refrain from seeking meanwhile an advantage at common law. [129] The recourse to arbitration was announced with the full agreement of both parties. This had been the position under Warham, who approved and encouraged the procedure in chancery and star chamber. [130] It was also Wolsey's endeavour to assist as many litigants as possible to end their suits by the independent award of arbitrators under the sanction of the king's council;

but, judging by the high proportion of failures to reach an award, the cardinal may sometimes have obtained initial consent by force of his personality rather than by the enthusiasm of litigants for settlement. On 10 July 1525, the suit between Ralph Leche and Sir John Savage for riot, forcible entry and title to the manor of Ilston, Derbyshire, was 'by the assent of bothe parties' committed to the arbitration of George Talbot, earl of Shrewsbury, Sir Anthony Fitzherbert and John Porte. The principals were then bound in £500 'to stand to and abide the ordre and awarde' of the arbitrators.[131] But a settlement was not possible: the earl and Sir Anthony twice moved Leche and Sir John to an award, but the latter 'wolde not aggree'. The arbitrators thus had no alternative but to certify Wolsey of their failure, and the suit resumed in star chamber with an unknown outcome.[132]

Early in 1527, a dispute between Thomas Grey, marquis of Dorset, and George lord Hastings concerning the exercising of certain offices was sent to arbitration. The parties were bound in £1000, each to the other, to abide a settlement and were injoined to command their servants meanwhile to show restraint in the disputed areas. This being a cause between leading councillors, the arbitrators named by the cardinal were himself, the duke of Norfolk, Sir Thomas Boleyn viscount Rochford, the two chief justices, the chief baron of the exchequer, Dr John Clerk, bishop of Bath, Sir Humphrey Coningsby and Sir Thomas More. Four, of whom Wolsey, Norfolk and the chief justice of the king's bench were to be three, constituted a *quorum*.[133] Settlement was to be reached by the last day of the Easter term, in order that the award might on that day be pronounced by the chancellor in the form of a final decree before the council in plenary session. Whether this actually happened cannot, unfortunately, be ascertained, owing to the loss of the Henrician council registers.

Arbitration might be arranged in town or country. After receiving their instructions from the council under authority of a writ of *dedimus potestatem,* the abbot of St Peter's, Gloucester, Sir Maurice Berkeley and Thomas Matson met representatives of the East and West parts of the forest of Dean in March 1520 to arbitrate on unspecified matters in controversy between them.[134] The parties quickly agreed on a proposed settlement and submitted themselves to abide a written 'arbytrement, or-dynaunce, award and judgement', which was to be delivered by the arbitrators on 17 April following. Each side was then bound in £400 to adhere to the settlement in every particular, the recognisances being post-dated to the day set for the inden-ture of the award.[135] Whether in town or country, it was the willing co-operation of the parties which provided the essential precondition for prompt settlement. The dispute between John Ap Howell and William Clay for alleged detinue of goods, which had first arrived in star chamber in 1522, was pending settlement for several years.[136] The arbitrators had difficulty in establishing the facts of the case because the defendant refused to make a true reckoning of his accounts. On 29 November 1529, they reported to Sir Thomas More that an agreement could not be reached; their belief was that Clay owed Ap Howell £800. Clay was brought before the council but stead-fastly refused to settle. He was therefore committed to prison by More's order 'for his obstinacy', and was to remain in-carcerated until he had made satisfaction to Ap Howell 'in money or wares' or 'otherwise agreed' with him.[137] A year later, however, the case was still unresolved.[138]

Perhaps most instructive as to the limitations of arbitration as a means to settlement is the suit which was in progress in star chamber from 1520 to 1526 between John Payne and Henry Lambert for title to land in Outwell, Norfolk.[139] Evidence was collected locally and this confirmed the plain-tiff's claim that the dispute turned on a dubious deed of release. Efforts to end the case by compromise before com-missioners in the country over a four year period had failed, and on 9 February 1524 the council ordered that a breviate of the suit should be prepared for the instruction of arbitrators named by Wolsey. Those initially appointed were Sir Richard Broke and William Ellis; the former was, however, replaced by Thomas Docwra. The parties were bound respectively in £100 to give their 'continuall attendance' in London 'untill the saide arbitrators have gyven their saide arbitrement'.[140] But the defendant was stubborn and the matter was still under consideration seventeen months later. Then, on 13 July 1525, the case began to move to a conclusion: Docwra sent word to Wolsey of the latest developments, and his messenger came next into star chamber, where the clerk of the council sat writing up his register in solitary state, to inform him that 'my lorde Cardinals pleasur' was that the recognisances requiring Payne and Lambert to remain in London should be vacated. [141] Docwra and Ellis had penetrated to the truth. It remained only to examine one Richard Prat – who languished in Dereham prison – on eight interrogatories.

When confirmation of the truth reached Wolsey, all thought of arbitration was dropped. The dispute was 'grett matter in conscyens'. [142] The deed of release from Payne to Lambert on which the issue turned had been extracted under duress. Since this was the very conclusion which had been arrived at by the first local commissioners appointed by Wolsey in 1520, it is somewhat surprising that arbitration had been considered thereafter. Perhaps, despite his reputation, Wolsey actually fought shy of the advance of equity? On 9 February 1526, however, the affairs of Outwell were finally debated in star chamber and the cardinal pronounced an equitable decree in favour of the plaintiff: Payne was to repay to Lambert five marks which had been given for the deed of release, and was 'to entre into the said mease and landes . . . and the same to have, hold, occupie and enjoye to hym and hys heires without interupcion of the said lambert or of hys heires'. [143] The plaintiff produced the five marks 'in open Corte . . . before the said moste Reverent fader in god and oder the said moste honorable councell', but the defendant refused to receive it. The money was therefore given to the deputy-warden of the Fleet for subsequent delivery to Lambert. [144]

The alternative route to settlement was that of extra-legal compromise, arrived at by the agreement of the parties to settle their differences after 'umpiring' by commissioners. Like arbitration, compromise by mediation might be attempted in town or country. On 10 July 1525, the dispute between John Coole and Piers Coryton was committed to Sir John Fitzjames and John Rowe 'to hear and examyn, and fynally to determyn or els to certifie'. [145] On 13 February 1527, the suit brought by John Colte against Richard Higham for title to goods was 'by their mutual assent' committed to Sir Richard Broke, Humphrey Brown and Henry Makwilliam to 'make an end' by mediation. If they were unable to do so, the cardinal had resolved 'to sett a fynall ende theryn by his order'. [146] Almost invariably, however, efforts at compromise were made in the locality of origin of the suit. There was no need for parties to plead special circumstances should they wish to join in commission to make an end by compromise before persons of repute in their county. The council actively encouraged – and later compelled – parties to attempt settlement by mediation. Commissions *ad audiendum et examinandum et finaliter determinandum,* authorised by writs of *dedimus potestatem,* were generally arranged after the parties were at issue, either before or after the examination of witnesses. Prior to Wolsey's 1526 policy of mandatory delegation, *ex parte* commissions were awarded only when the plaintiff expressed preference from the start for the procedure of local mediation to that of summoning the defendant before the council; in and after 1526, however, suits might be committed at any stage in their proceedings. [147]

The writ of *dedimus potestatem* gave the commissioners 'full powers' to hear and examine the matters in variance between the parties, and to set a final end to the dispute if they could. [148] If a settlement could not be reached, the commissioners were to report this to the council by a stated date in the following term. [149] The writ was attached to the bill of complaint, and any subsequent pleadings, proofs and other material necessary to the success of the hearing would be enclosed. The commissioners were instructed to return all documents to London should they be obliged to send in a certificate of their failure to effect a compromise. Certificates were to be in writing under seal and were to be engrossed on parchment. Many commissioners wrote out their certificates on the dorse of the bill of complaint. [150]

The commissioners appointed by the council would be the leading gentlemen, churchmen and other persons of status in the locality: they were members of the commission of the peace, bishops and abbots, members of the commission for the subsidy or otherwise office-holders. On 4 July 1525, an unquiet title to land at Lyneham Heath, Oxfordshire, was committed to the abbot of Oseney, Sir Edward Chamberlain, William Fermour and Sir Thomas Elyot.[151] On 7 February 1527, a similar suit arising in Staffordshire was committed to Sir Anthony Fitzherbert, Sir John Gifford and the abbot of Burton-on-Trent.[152] Local persons such as these were likely to know the parties and the particular matters in dispute, and had social as well as personal authority. In Wales and the marches and (after 1525) in the northern counties, local commissioners could be drawn from the personnel of the provincial councils.

The council, in its increasing need under Wolsey to reduce its arrears of judicial work at the centre, was greatly hopeful that cases might be peacefully ended if the parties came together under the supervision of local 'umpires'.[153] On the more positive side too, the development of extra-legal compromise reflected Wolsey's undying conviction that all that was needed to settle relatively trivial suits was common sense and a little give and take on both sides. The cardinal, therefore, found it difficult to understand why the procedure appeared so unsuccessful at ending litigation. Lack of success stemmed first from the fact that consent to the verdict of the umpires was required from *both* parties for that verdict to be good. Secondly, the decision of commissioners was not in reality final even if accepted, since it was not legally binding. Decisions founded on common sense could always be controverted by learned argument. A little give and take was a fine thing, so long as one was ever taking, never giving!

Many commissioners appointed to hear and end suits were thus obliged to certify to similar effect.

For asmoche as we betwen the same parties could make none fynall determynacion in the matter in varyaunce dependying betwen theym, we therfor . . . send onto your grace and oder lordes of the kinges most honorable Counsaill the byll of Complaynt and thanswer, and the said deposycions, with the said Commyssyon in this our certificat inclosed, assigned and sealyd with our handes.[154]

This lack of success was only very rarely the result of the incompetence or procrastination of the commissioners.[155] It was the conduct of the litigants themselves that was the cause of failure. If a litigant thought that the 'umpires' were not of his part, he would obstruct proceedings or desire remission to London.[156] If he perceived from the evidence that he had a weak case, he would withdraw his co-operation and demand dismissal to the common law.[157] An ingenious defendant might frustrate a commission by successfully obtaining a writ of *supersedeas* out of chancery.[158] But in most instances of failure, the commissioners were unable to mediate because the parties obstinately refused to settle.[159] In these circumstances, the commissioners referred suits back to Westminster, giving the parties their day of appearance in star chamber and informing the council of this in their certificate.

It should in fairness be noted that the system was such that a successful settlement by compromise would in theory leave no trace in the records at the centre. In practice, commissioners appear to have sent in certificates to London whatever the outcome; nevertheless, a scientific evaluation of the efficacy of commissions *ad audiendum et examinandum et finaliter determinandum* is not possible. It may be that the certificate most representative of the real situation was that of Nicholas West, bishop of Ely, the abbot of Bury St Edmunds, William Ellis and Sir Robert Clere, to whom Wolsey had directed a commission to hear and end a bundle of East Anglian suits. The commissioners called the parties before them and peacefully ended most of the cases 'according to good order of law, right in good Conscience'. It was true that they could not end those cases which were at the suit of Thomas Codlyng. Codlyng had entirely ignored the precepts of the commissioners, having 'no more Regard to the saide byshop of Ely than he had to the strawe under his Foote'.[160] Some cases were, however, settled in the country[161] – but for how long? The dispute between William Bingham and Thomas Palmer for title to a mill and nearby land in Northamptonshire had been committed to the

mediation of four 'honest, discret and indifferent personnes' in
the locality. The commissioners proposed 'a fynall determynacion, concorde and end', and this was accepted by the parties.
Yet, shortly afterwards, Palmer – who had done well out of the
settlement – had been persuaded to sell his title to two third
parties, Anthony Busterde and one Weston. These men then
maintained Palmer to 'move complaint' to defeat Bingham's
interest before the council in the white hall, whence Palmer
successfully obtained a commission for the examination of
witnesses addressed to none other than Busterde and his
friends. Busterde then summoned Palmer alone of the parties
before him 'in a forreyne countie', so-called 'witnesses' led by
Weston were examined, and the 'evidence' collected was
engrossed on parchment and sent up to London, whither
Palmer no doubt hastened to move the council for an early
hearing. The scheme was unsubtle and it did not work. The incident nevertheless illuminates what might happen to a suit
after a supposedly final settlement. [162]

When at last the civil suits which had not fallen asleep *en
route,* or been compromised out of court, reached determination in star chamber, the decision was confirmed in the form of
a decree. In the absence of the Henrician council registers, it is
impossible to discover how many suits – civil or criminal – actually did reach this final stage and on what grounds. From the
scraps of material which are extant in draft or transcript, it
would appear that relatively few private litigants had the
satisfaction of seeing their cases ended by a judgment, even if
that decision was no more than the pronouncement of an expert opinion or a settlement by arbitration. It would also seem
that, to reach a decree, litigants had to persist, even to the extent – like Helier de Carteret, bailiff of Jersey – of interrupting
a plenary session of the council by thrusting through the en-
trance to star chamber and crying out to Wolsey, 'Sir, I beg
and entreat you to give me justice.' Carteret claimed that he
had waited in London for three years by the express command
of the cardinal: 'and all this time I have not been able to get
a hearing'. The bailiff then complained that Wolsey kept
him out of his manor and office 'by sequestration' and all his

money was spent. 'I am a poor gentleman burdened with a
wife and children . . .; consider then, Sir, if I have reason to
speak or not.' No doubt Carteret had embellished his story
when he returned home to Jersey. His try-on, nevertheless,
worked and he got his decree.[163] Others were not so fortunate.
Unluckiest of all may have been those litigants who had been
the victims of stubbornly uncompromising opponents before
local commissioners. When these suits were referred back to
the centre, the cardinal had a habit of bundling them up and
despatching them to the white hall for further hearing before
the dean of the chapel royal and his associates.[164]

As to the grounds on which star chamber suits might come
to a decree, these may have varied from chancellor to
chancellor. Decrees which incorporated the results of a
successful arbitration or an agreement to settle made between
the parties at the centre and submitted to the council for approval and confirmation were common to all chancellors.
Otherwise, both Warham and Wolsey were keen to ensure that
the council in star chamber maintained fully its traditional
reputation for equitable proceedings, good conscience and the
punishment of wrongdoers. The former had taken enormous
pains in providing a solution to a complex suit concerning
carriers who broke bulk.[165] The latter was willing to protect
the beneficial interests of the *cestui que use,* while injoining the
son and heir of the deceased enfeoffor to do no violence and
make no entry until such time as he had recovered at common
law.[166] Wolsey also pronounced decrees in 1520 and 1523 for
the protection of the leases and customary rights enjoyed by
the tenants of Holland during the nonage of the third earl of
Derby, the earl having succeeded to title, even though to do so
was contrary to a clear legal interest. The decrees were in the
interests of fairness but, as their author readily admitted, were
against the 'rigour' of the common law.[167] Sometimes, indeed,
it seems as though Warham and Wolsey saw no distinction
between their roles in chancery and star chamber. It would be
interesting to know how the judges and sergeants-at-law
reacted to this: perhaps they saw no distinction either? Sir
Thomas More, for his part, preferred stricter arrangements in

star chamber when chancellor, determining unquiet titles only in accordance with legal opinion.[168] He nevertheless showed consideration for all serious points of view, being particularly concerned to protect third parties from the effects of disruptive real property litigation.[169] Sir Thomas Audley was probably the least flexible of the early Tudor chancellors. His greatest concern was for the 'right and true meaning' of the law.[170] If his sympathies were ever with the development of the courts of equitable jurisdiction, he did his best to disguise the fact.

Decrees were pronounced in star chamber by the lord chancellor, being 'enacted' and 'adjudged' by him and the other lords of the council. As the chancellor spoke, the clerk of the council took scribbled notes which were drafted into the proper form later.[171] Alternatively a decree might be drawn by counsel for the successful party; he handed his rendering of the chancellor's pronouncement to the clerk, who checked it against his notes and made any necessary alterations.[172] If determination was before an *ad hoc* committee of councillors, a decree would be given verbal publication in the name of the council by the senior councillor present.[173] All decrees, however made or drawn, were then entered into the current council register.[174] As historians have noted, a number of the decrees pronounced by Wolsey in star chamber extolled the personal supremacy of the cardinal at the council board.[175] The decree usually cited[176] is nonetheless extant in a polished form: the commentator should be prepared to share the amusement which Richard Eden, clerk of the council, evidently took in drafting exotic texts which read as hybrid versions of a royal charter and a papal bull – all in the name of a former butcher's son. When a decree was entered in the register, the parties could obtain copies from the clerk. Copies were, when possible, signed by the lord chancellor and those of the council who were present when the decree was made.[177] The 'original' text was, however, the one entered in the register. If required, successful parties could obtain exemplifications of their decrees under the great seal in the form of letters patent.[178] The council might itself order the enrolment of a decree in the chancery and instruct the parties to obtain exemplifications to be kept in their respective possessions, in order that none should pretend 'ignorance of the same'.[179] The record of a decree was also, where necessary, transferable by writ of *mittimus*.[180]

The phraseology of the surviving drafts and transcripts indicates that the council contemplated varying degrees of finality in the making of its decrees, according to the circumstances in which a suit stood at the time of pronouncement. Some decrees did not exclude the possibility of further order at some future date, or awarded possession to a party with the added proviso that the other party might begin new proceedings at law. Even the decree in Payne's case, which initially described itself as 'final', later conceded that the decision could be reversed if Lambert successfully established 'by evidens, witnes or oderwise' before the council that he 'hath better right and title, aswell in Constiens as in lawe and good equite to the premisses'.[181] If the council wished to be especially emphatic, it would exclude all provisos and demand that the unsuccessful party 'sease and relynquysse' forthwith all litigation elsewhere for the same matter either at law or equity.[182]

After a successful suit, the fortunate litigant set off for home with his costs in his purse and his decree in his pocket.[183] Unfortunately, a decree was not necessarily the same as satisfaction, and the council had a poor record in terms of finality of decrees in civil suits.[184] Nevertheless, the council was not oblivious to the problem of enforcement and the parties might — if not already bound as in arbitration — be required to enter into recognisances in sums varying from £100 to £1000 to observe a decree.[185] In suits for goods and chattels, commissioners might be appointed to assess the value of the items and to ensure either redelivery or the payment of adequate compensation.[186] Nor was a successful litigant without some remedy if his opponent elected to lie in prison rather than obey the council's decree. A writ of execution might be directed to the sheriff to put a party in possession or to levy costs and damages, if awarded, on the lands and goods of a defeated litigant.[187] The council was also willing to order sequestration.[188] Ultimately, parties refusing to obey the council's decrees became liable to process of contempt and imprisonment in the Fleet.[189]

LITIGANTS AND LITIGATION

Private litigation was both expensive and time-consuming. It is therefore not surprising to discover that the litigants who appeared before the council in star chamber were members of the higher and wealthier ranks of society. Analysis of the 'definite' Wolsey suits[190] with extant proceedings in which the social status of the parties is given (table 2) indicates that the principals to litigation were almost invariably gentlemen, beneficed clergy, officials, merchants, or prosperous yeomen or husbandmen.

Table 2

Status	Plaintiffs	Defendants
Gentleman and above	216 (28.7%)	533 (35.1%)
Clergy	131 (17.4%)	143 (9.4%)
Officer	49 (6.5%)	114 (7.5%)
Professional	15 (2.0%)	30 (2.0%)
Merchant	74 (9.8%)	113 (7.5%)
Yeoman/Husbandman	191 (25.4%)	386 (25.5%)
Craftsman	43 (5.7%)	91 (6.0%)
Labourer	11 (1.5%)	82 (5.4%)
Pauper	2 (0.3%)	1 (0.1%)
Other	21 (2.7%)	22 (1.5%)
Total	753 (100%)	1515 (100%)

Social status of principals

In only two cases under Wolsey was the plaintiff allowed to sue without charge *in forma pauperis.*[191] No doubt pauper plaintiffs were expected to take their suits to the dean of the chapel royal.

Litigants came to star chamber from all parts of the country. The geographical distribution of the extant cases suggests that proximity to London, the size and comparative wealth of a county and its immediate local conditions were closely related to the number of incipient disputes which became cases before the council. London with Middlesex, Kent, Surrey, Hampshire, Sussex, Essex and Hertfordshire all provided a high aggregate of cases. Yorkshire and Lincolnshire – the largest counties – yielded many suits. Litigation from the West Country, especially Devon and Cornwall, reflected relative prosperity and economic growth, but also the disturbed state of these counties. The contribution of Norfolk and Suffolk was also considerable. East Anglia was responsible for most of the enclosure cases in star chamber, and it is also evident that a number of petitions which were delivered to Wolsey at the time of his pilgrimage to Walsingham were heard before the council when the cardinal returned to London. [192]

Vexatious litigants remained a constant problem, but the council seemed unable to devise effective machinery for the discouragement of frivolous suits. As Jones observes, gentlemen 'who talked as easily of the law as of their crops were all too capable of talking down their advisers; they did not ask whether to proceed so much as how to proceed'. [193] No doubt the majority of suitors genuinely aimed to secure redress of a wrong in one court or another, but a substantial minority desired to harass the opposing party or at least to cause him inconvenience and expense. Many litigants planned the strategies of litigation themselves. Lawyers, as a result, were frequently expected to dress the case to suit the client's requirements. In all circumstances, star chamber was an attractive proposition. This was an awesome court and one that was hard on defendants. Moreover, during Wolsey's years, it was served by a lord chancellor who appeared to be actually encouraging litigation. The wide jurisdiction of the council enabled much to be made out of next to nothing, by generous interpretation of any violent aspects of the matter in question, whether recent or not so recent. Finally, the facility under Wolsey to obtain the issue of a writ of *subpoena* before filing a

bill of complaint meant that the plaintiff need not have devised
the charges before the day set for the defendant's appearance.

The genesis of a frivolous suit can be clearly traced from certain events in Shrewsbury on 28 May 1516. [194] William
Gyttyns, a local landowner, and Thomas Trentham, a
gentleman farmer, had a small matter between them. Gyttyns
claimed an annual rent of 13s 4d for a mese and 6s for a gar-
den. Trentham was not disposed to pay, and the trifle seems to
have concealed an unquiet title. It was decided to put the
matter to the award of independent local third parties. On 28
May, before the decision of the arbitrators, the two men met in
the local tavern, 'The Gullet', where Gyttyns was describing
for the edification of those present the new horse he had
bought that day. The pot was refilled with wine, and Gyttyns
and Trentham drank together. Said Gyttyns, 'I am coming to
drink with thee albeit that we be in law together', and
Trentham replied, 'Gyttyns, it is told me that thou hast accused me at London.' To this the landowner declared without
inhibition that, had not his friends restrained him, he would
have accused Trentham before the king's council. At this
Trentham drew his dagger and a brawl ensued. No damage
was done, however, except that Gyttyns had his clothes torn.
He departed home, somewhat deflated, leaving his opponent
to finish the wine. That evening Trentham called at Gyttyns's
house, as he later claimed to apologise for his behaviour; but
nothing was done, since Gyttyns saw him coming and barred
the door. When Trentham knocked, there was no reply. He
waited, and then called next door on Gyttyns's neighbour,
where he remained for two hours, partaking of further refresh-
ment, after which he went home. Gyttyns, however, resolved to
make something of the matter, and rode to London. There he
took legal advice with a view to a suit in star chamber. His bill
of complaint was a model of its type. Counsel provided expertise and explained the form; Gyttyns provided the material
and the embellishments. The bill was then drawn. It consisted
of accusations of riot, retaining and assault, clearly concocted
out of the events in the ale-house; as a result of these outrages,
Gyttyns's wife, who was pregnant and nearing her time, gave

birth prematurely through fear and lay long in 'jeopardy' of her life. The bill concluded with a fulsome recital of alleged local corruption, in which Trentham played villain. As a principal cause of much litigation which arrived in the cardinal's court, the dishonesty of litigants can be paralleled only by the chancellor's own naivety; while offering increased facilities for judicial business at the council board, Wolsey failed to curtail the many opportunities for vexatious suits and abuse of procedure.

The professionals who aided litigants were counsel and the two attorneys in star chamber. Counsel (sergeants-at-law and barristers) were engaged from the start and were consulted for advice on the drawing of pleadings and interrogatories, although they were principally employed to argue the case at hearings after publication. The attorneys handled all procedural details. In all, the activity of sixty-nine counsellors-at-the-bar can be detected in star chamber under Wolsey.[195] Four barristers in particular specialised in star chamber work and built up extensive practices: they were Robert Chydley (Inner Temple), John Densell (Lincoln's Inn), John Hynde (Gray's Inn), and John Orenge (Middle Temple).[196] It was under the cardinal that the position of the two attorneys in star chamber became established. In the reign of Henry VII, it had been possible for a litigant to appoint any convenient person to be his attorney.[197] This was not so in the time of Henry VIII. By Wolsey's general order in 1527, most defendants were admitted to attorney after examination as a matter of course;[198] this measure appears to have been that which assured the future of the two professional attorneys of the 1520s, John Valentine and William Mill.[199] It was not the case that one attorney represented the plaintiff and the other the defendant; no rule applied and either attorney might be selected.[200] In the 1530s, an attorney could expect to be retained in a minimum of twenty-one suits per term.[201] Once appointed, the attorney represented the client in court and briefed the client's counsel. The attorneys were also employed by the clerk of the council to copy pleadings at his direction. They were not, however, regarded as 'clerks of office' prior to

the reign of Elizabeth.[202] William Mill served in star chamber
as an attorney from *c.* 1520 to the reign of Mary, when he was
succeeded by his son William, the future clerk of the court.[203]
John Valentine was succeeded in *c.* 1535 by John Taverner.[204]

The length of litigation in star chamber, as in most sixteenth-century courts, was conditioned by the inclinations of
the litigants to speedy determination as much as by procedural
difficulties. Due process, however, generally meant slow
process, especially in cases involving legal opinion. In the
absence of the council registers, it is not possible to generalise,
and evidence for the longevity of litigation is sparse. Standards
of comparison with other courts are also lacking. However, as
far as can be estimated from the extant proceedings, and ignoring for the purpose the council's record in terms of finality of
decrees, it appears that the majority of suits required one year
to pass through all their formal stages from bill of complaint to
determination.[205] Some cases took less and others more. The
cause célèbre waged between the prior of Norwich and the city
lasted for thirty-two years.[206] Suits which involved unquiet
titles were most prone to longevity. The case between the
Fleming family and Patrick Bellew lasted at least three
decades in star chamber, and was in progress throughout
Wolsey's ascendancy.[207] The shortest extant case took just one
term to progress from bill of complaint to a final decree.[208] The
decree authorised the earl of Worcester to hold sessions in eyre
within the lordship of Gower, and commanded the tenants and
inhabitants to give their attendance. Both these extremes illustrate features of star chamber litigation. The Norwich and
Fleming cases betray obtuse thinking, repetition of claims and
the stubbornness of litigants. The earl of Worcester's case ex-
poses the speed and efficiency of an administrative body sitting
as a court.[209]

The council was particularly inclined to exert propulsion in
criminal suits. In Davenport's case, where the defendants were
accused of aiding and abetting felony by spiriting one Robert
Pownall out of Cheshire into Lancashire after an unpleasant
murder, the depositions of witnesses had been taken in star
chamber precisely two months after the crime itself was

committed.[210] Sir Robert Constable, charged by Ralph
Rokeby with the abduction of a ward on 15 April 1524, had
been examined and had submitted to the council's order by the
first week of the ensuing Trinity term.[211] But as a rule, and in
civil suits, it was necessary to allow six months for mesne
process and the answer and examination of the defendant.[212] A
further six months were required to progress to a hearing and a
decree, assuming that the case remained at the centre.[213]

The expenses of litigation were closely related to the length
of the proceedings. Basic costs were the termly fees required to
retain counsel (3s 4d) and an attorney (20d).[214] The cost of
written pleadings and interrogatories depended on their
length, but most documents were longer than could be obtained for the minimum charges. Counsel's minimum fee for
drawing an instrument would be 3s 4d, plus 1s for 'making the
same in parchment' in his office.[215] Fees then had to be paid in
court for process and to the clerk: for a writ of *subpoena* or attachment (2s 6d), for a privy seal summons (7s), for a writ of
dedimus potestatem (3s 4d); for the entry of the appearance of
every person and for admission to attorney (each 2s); for the
entry and warrant for process or a commission (2s), for an
affidavit (1s 8d), for the copy of a pleading (1s minimum), for
the examination of every witness (2s), and for an injunction
(5s); for drawing a recognisance (6s 8d) or a decree (4s
minimum), and the entry of the same (1s 4d minimum).[216]
Counsel's court fees were incurred at the rate of 3s 4d per
day.[217] The costs, where necessary, of hiring process-servers
were additional.[218] Such charges were genuine. Less authentic
were the expenses alleged for board and lodging in London
and journeys to and from the provinces. William Tunstall, for
example, claimed £8 for legal advice and court fees, and £40 for
six expeditions from Lancaster to London at £6 13s 4d per
journey.[219]

Bills of costs were submitted to the council by successful
parties or their attorneys at the conclusion of suits, and the
costs to be awarded against the losers were taxed by the lord
chancellor.[220] It was not usual to meet claims in full: Margery
Warford's costs of £6 1s 8d were taxed by Wolsey at £3 6s

6d.[221] In frivolous suits, however, full costs would be allowed: Robert Dyllon's costs of £5 19s 4d were taxed at £6.[222] The expenses claimed had, nevertheless, to be reasonable. In Richard Malkin's case (a frivolous suit), the cardinal refused to accept a bill for 'horsemete and mansmete', and alleged expenses of £2 10s 4d were taxed at £1 6s 8d.[223] In his assessment of costs, the chancellor would take into account previous litigation on the same subject. William Tunstall claimed £9 for his costs 'at two sessions at Lancaster'.[224] Other litigants obtained their expenses in chancery prior to a suit in star chamber.[225] Costs might thus amount to substantial sums: Helier de Carteret was awarded £40.[226] Not every unsuccessful party could pay on demand. On 20 July 1517 John Cole was bound by recognisance in 100 marks to pay £50 costs in two equal instalments at Michaelmas 1517 and 1518.[227] Those who simply refused to pay would be imprisoned; nor was refusal any use since costs were recoverable by the sheriff of the county.[228]

Damages were not frequently awarded by the council. When they were a usual amount in criminal cases was £10 for assault, battery or false imprisonment.[229] The successful party in civil suits made a claim for damages when finalising his bill of costs. William Tunstall claimed £111 10s 8d for corn wrongfully taken from his manor, which was probably excessive.[230] Thomas Dawes, adding together the value of his lost 'panniers', his charges in the Marshalsea and other 'wrongful vexation', asked for £10 8s.[231] Where necessary, the council would order that damages were to be levied by the sheriff. On 6 June 1519, Wolsey awarded Richard Brokebanck damages of £500 against the merchants of the Steelyard. If any delay was made in the 'execution of this decree', the sheriffs of London were to be commanded by writ to raise the *posse comitatus* and to levy the damages by force if necessary.[232] On 2 July following, however, the merchants brought the £500 into star chamber.[233]

Costs and damages, when awarded, would be accompanied in criminal and quasi-criminal suits by a fine.[234] Fines were not regularly imposed by the early Tudor council except for contempt: suits which were in reality criminal remained in a minority until the mid-sixteenth century. The evidence is not substantial, owing to the loss of the Henrician council registers, but it appears that the amounts of fines assessed after private suits in star chamber ranged from 20 shillings to 500 marks.[235] The usual sums were £5 or £10.[236] In Hilary term 1517 at least three fines were imposed. Thomas Trentham paid £5 for contempt, Sir Walter Calverley was fined £10 for riot and £10 for contempt, and John Copinger's fine (for abduction) was assessed at 100 marks.[237] In Hilary term 1518, Thomas Hewet and Edmund Ball were each fined £5 for a riot at Thetford and were bound by recognisance in £40 to make payment in two equal instalments.[238] On 30 November 1518, Sir William Brereton indented for a fine of 500 marks for 'comforting' felons.[239] Brereton was obliged to covenant with the cardinal, Sir Thomas Lovell (treasurer of the household) and Sir John Heron (treasurer of the chamber) to pay the sum by twice-yearly instalments of 50 marks. Sir William was also required for 'sure payment thereof' to permit the fictitious recovery of a group of his manors in the court of common pleas. If he defaulted in his instalments, the cardinal and his co-recoverers would automatically stand seised to the use of the king.[240] The actions for 'recovery' duly took place.[241] Ultimately, however, the fine was discharged.

Fines were collected in three ways. The first method was the simplest: the offender paid the money into star chamber.[242] Alternatively the record of a fine was estreated into the exchequer; the money was then either paid direct to the tellers in the exchequer of receipt or levied as a debt due to the king.[243] By 1550 the estreat of star chamber fines into the exchequer had become the accepted procedure.[244] Prior to 1530, however, large fines were invariably paid direct to the treasurer of the chamber.[245] As in Sir William Brereton's case, indentures or obligations were drawn which recorded the extent of the liability and the details concerning payment; copies were then sent to the treasurer of the chamber, and the record was enrolled in chancery.[246] When the required sums were paid, the record was cancelled.[247] Large or small fines might be paid by instalments.[248] In the case of a small offender, the party would usually be bound in his own recognisance to pay specified sums on specified days.[249] Sureties might, however, be required to guarantee payment.[250]

In certain cases, the council ordered imprisonment or other punishment in lieu of, or in addition to, a fine. Imprisonment was a recognised punishment in the early Tudor period for contempt of the council's process and its orders and decrees, and for perjury in the council chamber.[251] The delinquent would be committed to the Fleet until he submitted and the contempt was purged. Otherwise imprisonment tended to be confined to the most serious criminal cases: felony and abduction, riot, unlawful assembly and rescue were rewarded by incarceration in the Tower, the Marshalsea or the more lenient (but expensive) Fleet.[252] Wolsey's chancellorship saw in addition the development of alternative punishments for the lower orders of society, mainly the pillory and the wearing of papers, the latter often while riding a horse but facing the tail.[253] The cucking-stool was used, and men seem not to have escaped this punishment.[254] Wolsey could also be more severe. On 14 October 1519, Robert Dunkell was 'adjudged' to be set upon the newly-erected pillory in the palace of Westminster. One of his ears was to be nailed to the structure until nightfall, when it was to be pulled away 'yf he liste'; the unfortunate Dunkell was then to be banished the realm.[255] In punishments as well as due process, therefore, the cardinal's court presaged the star chamber of the later sixteenth and the seventeenth centuries.

5

Impact and Achievement

THE CARDINAL

The assessment of Thomas Wolsey's achievement in star chamber rests on an evaluation of the importance and success of his management of the council there. As to the impact of his policy of enforcement, which had been unveiled before the king and council in May 1516, the cardinal was himself in no doubt; and ignoring the minister's 'orations' in star chamber, his vainglorious boasting and the uncritical admiration of sycophants, there was truth in the claim. Wolsey gave the council's enforcement function a renewed impetus, beginning by imposing reformation on the lay aristocracy and the king's councillors. As we have seen, the earl of Northumberland, the marquis of Dorset, George lord Hastings, lord Burgavenny and Sir Richard Sacheverell learnt of the practical execution of the cardinal's plan within weeks of its announcement. [1]

The implementation of the policy was not, however, confined to a burst of energy in the early years of Wolsey's chancellorship. In a list of matters to be taken in council compiled in the autumn of 1519, the 'egall and Indifferent administracion of Justice' still headed the agenda, taking priority over the reform of the exchequer, the affairs of Ireland, the suppression of idleness and the fortification of the borders.[2] Concern continuously extended to the demeanour of local magistrates (justifiably), and all justices of the peace were encouraged to attend annually in star chamber to be 'new sworn', prior to the swearing-in of the sheriffs.[3] Those who could not appear in person were sworn by means of commissions of *dedimus potestatem,* the commissioners including an assize judge whose circuit embraced the relevant county.[4] At the ceremony in star chamber itself, a homily was read that would have emphasised the passage in the justice's oath which required the doing of 'egall right to the poore and to the rich'.[5] It is clear, however, that Wolsey visualised a two-way relationship between central government and its servants in the localities: on 5 July 1526, as many commissioners of the peace and of the subsidy as could conveniently be assembled were obliged to attend on the cardinal in star chamber.[6] There, after a preliminary 'oration', one hundred and ten J.P.s were commanded to certify their answers to twenty-one articles of inquiry concerning the prevalence of offences against justice in their localities.[7] The episode is known only from the Ellesmere extracts, but it obviously represented a further step towards the development in England of a public investigatory and prosecutional function to combat crime, a function firmly allocated to the justices of the peace by the Marian statutes.[8] A second inquiry, concerning vagabondage and associated delinquency, was combined with the corn survey proclaimed on 12 November 1527.[9] Thomas Howard, duke of Norfolk, proved particularly active as a commissioner in East Anglia: thieves, coiners and vagabonds were apprehended and imprisoned, pilloried or reported to the centre.[10] Writing to Wolsey, the duke expressed the opinion that many more offenders would be identified if the leaders of those already taken were racked in the Tower. But, as always, the use of torture required the king's licence which Norfolk did not have.[11] The certificates of the commissioners appointed to undertake the survey were received by the council in star chamber in December 1527 and early in 1528.[12] The duke of Norfolk had suggested the issue of commissions of gaol delivery to empty such prisons as had been filled by the survey commissioners, and this was done in January and February 1528.[13] Those in custody were therefore dealt with in accordance with accepted legal procedure.

By the last years of the cardinal's office, the effect of the policy of enforcement had been felt as far north as the West Riding, where Wolsey had transformed the composition of the commission of the peace. The number of local gentry appointed to the commission had been reduced between 1513 and 1525 from a dominant twenty-nine to fifteen; the number of lay outsiders was increased from five to fifteen.[14] The disappearance of men like Sir Richard Tempest of Bolling and Sir William Gascoigne of Gawthorpe from the commission can only have been the result of deliberate planning, and in some cases the newcomers had specific connections with Wolsey, notably Sir William Gascoigne of Cardington (Bedfordshire), the treasurer of the cardinal's household and 'a right politique man'.[15]

It was also under the cardinal that Sir Richard Tempest, Sir Henry Savile, Sir William Gascoigne and Sir Robert Constable in Yorkshire, the Stanley dynasty in Lancashire, the Brereton family in Chester, Sir John Savage the elder in Worcestershire and others first learned the 'law of the star chamber', even if only as defendants in private suits. The difficulty of obtaining justice before the commissions of the peace had caused men with grievances and sufficient money to travel to take their cases into star chamber, 'wher the complaynauntes shal not drede to shewe the trouthe of thair grefe'.[16] The government's enforced reliance on unsupervised local nobles was an administrative defect which Wolsey had it in hand to reform. In Lancashire, Thomas Stanley, second earl of Derby, had himself been the greatest threat to good order.[17] His military following enabled the earl to impose his own government in his territory. He issued proclamations in his name, he and his retainers were favoured by the justices at Lancaster, and the earl's opponents claimed of Sir Henry Marney that they could have but little redress even from the chancellor of the duchy.[18] Failure to obey royal writs and commissions was a common occurrence in Lancashire, and attacks on officials were frequent. Corruption, extortion and the petty rivalries of local gentry were the constant impediment to effective rule from Westminster in the outlying counties.

Wolsey took particular interest in the affairs of the north. As archbishop of York he remained a dominant power and influence there, even though he did not enter his diocese until shortly before his death.[19] Within the archbishop's own jurisdiction, Beverley and Hexham were threatened with the curtailment of their 'accustomed' liberties by *quo warranto,* should they not abandon their tradition of lawlessness and duly present rioters and other offenders before the justices of the peace.[20] The mayor of York was deposed and the city reduced to humbly thanking Wolsey that it was to remain a city.[21] In star chamber, a record was at one point kept of the 'misdemeanours, enormyties, injuries and wrongs' done within Yorkshire which remained 'unreformed' by the cardinal.[22] Several of the offences noted in the document pertained to the activities of the fifth earl of Northumberland: it had not been insignificant that the earl had been the first to be humbled in 1516.

On 16 July 1524, Wolsey appointed special commissioners to inquire into the administration of justice and to reform 'enormities' in Yorkshire and Northumberland.[23] The commissioners, led by the duke of Norfolk who was being sent to the northern marches as lieutenant-general for the second time in two years, sat at York on 30 July and at Newcastle-upon-Tyne about 10 August.[24] The duke sent in his report to Wolsey, and in early October the cardinal found time to congratulate Norfolk on his 'greate endevour' for justice.[25] Serious complaints had been made against Thomas lord Dacre of Gillesland, who had held the office of warden of all the marches since 1511,[26] both to the duke and to John Kite, bishop of Carlisle, and Wolsey resolved to investigate them in star chamber.[27] When Dacre appeared at Westminster, the council debated charges which included 'remissness and negligence' and 'bearinge of Theaves'. The warden promptly submitted, signed a confession and was imprisoned in the

Fleet.[28] How long he remained there is unknown, but on 1 and 6 September 1525, he compounded in 1,500 marks for his maladministration of justice in the north and entered into a series of recognisances for his future behaviour.[29] The warden was bound in 5,000 marks to his appearance in star chamber at any time upon twenty days' notice given by the council, and was to 'content' those injured by his misfeasance. Dacre's rule in the north had been undisguisedly partial and was potentially disastrous to the development of Tudor government;[30] his sole qualification for office had been his military following, 'redy at hande to withstande excourses to be made by the Scottes from tyme to tyme'.[31] That the warden should have been brought to account and punished in star chamber was a major triumph for Wolsey's policy of enforcement: the event marked the end of the age of the medieval robber baron. Dacre was dead within two months of his submission.[32] His death resulted in a feud between his son, William, and Henry Clifford, earl of Cumberland, over the office of warden of the west marches obtained by the latter.[33] The power vacuum had, however, already been filled by Wolsey's reconstruction of conciliar government in the north during June and July 1525.[34]

As lord chancellor, therefore, Wolsey acted resolutely to establish and maintain the king's peace and the impartial administration of justice throughout his realm, using the council in star chamber as a wedge to force back local privilege and abuse. The motives behind particular actions at the centre might sometimes carry sinister or political overtones, as after the Hunne affair; they were, however, no more questionable than the motives of Henry VII and his intimate councillors, in whose hands enforcement measures invariably carried fiscal implications. We may not share Pollard's euphoria when speaking of Wolsey's policy,[35] but nor may we accept Elton's criticism that the evidence for the cardinal's concern to enforce justice on the overmighty is 'slight'.[36] Wolsey's efforts were real if but a beginning, sustained if somewhat haphazardly directed. That the extant documentation is slender is surely due to the loss of the main series of council *acta* for the period. The essence of the policy was the better enforcement of the law in the existing courts of common law, with the assignment to the council in star chamber of a firm supervisory and, if necessary, punitive role, thus ensuring the efficient application and impartial administration of the system. No Tudor chancellor could improve on Wolsey's overall design, and the development of star chamber continued steadily on the lines the cardinal had laid down.

As to the second aspect of the cardinal's management of the council, Wolsey appears to have remained generally convinced that his popularisation of the council courts was a great public benefit, despite recurrent spells of disillusion. The facility of free access for suitors to the council was in part a necessary consequence of the promulgation of the enforcement policy. Better enforcement clearly depended on conciliar supervision; the council, for its part, was almost entirely dependent upon the information it received from individuals. The popularisation of the council courts also reflected the cardinal's genuine concern for the poor and oppressed, a sentiment appropriate both to churchman and lord chancellor. But Wolsey could be impatient and erratic; he did, from time to time, live up to his reputation for cavalier treatment of litigants and litigation. There was, for example, his reception of George Bayen's suit against William Underhill in 1527. [37] After hopeless litigation in king's bench, common pleas and the white hall, Bayen came before the cardinal in star chamber to try out his luck. Wolsey was easily fooled and the plaintiff praised him as a 'noble judge'. The defendant, who initially refused to appear, was successfully attached in 1529, and a day was set for a final hearing in the ensuing Michaelmas term. Wolsey's fall intervened. The plaintiff therefore made suit to the new chancellor in Hilary term 1530, but received in reply what Sir Thomas More – after scrutiny – regarded as a fully justified rebuff. Was the cardinal a plaintiffs' judge as well as a litigants' chancellor? If he was indeed retailing the justice of star chamber without sufficient consideration of the relative merits of the complaints brought before him or the honesty of the aspiring litigants, the action of his successor in office was considerably more responsible.

A second insight was provided by the bill of Isabel Adams, Christine Hawken and Agnes Page, filed in More's chancellorship.[38] The plaintiffs' husbands had initiated litigation in star chamber under Warham and Wolsey against the abbot of Bury St Edmunds, concerning land disputed between the abbey and the town, but the suit had never been ended because the abbot had always avoided his opponents' demands that he should show his deeds of title. At the time of Wolsey's visit to Bury *en route* for Walsingham, however, the abbot had taken up the case with the chancellor in advantageous circumstances. On hearing the abbot's account, according to the plaintiffs, the cardinal had committed their husbands to prison without a hearing, and the leading inhabitants of Bury were compelled to swear on the gospels that they would discontinue their suit against the abbey in perpetuity. Wolsey had never ordered the release of the husbands, and the plaintiffs begged More for this, and that the inhabitants of Bury should be summoned to declare in truth what 'direction' the cardinal had made regarding the dispute between the abbey and the town. The usual discounts must be allowed for exaggeration but the questions remain: did Wolsey sometimes lack discrimination and could he be swayed by *ex parte* argument? Allegations of improper conduct were all too easily made against judges who were inclined to follow their instincts or make decisions without hearing both sides of a case.

The defect in Wolsey's approach to litigation and in his scheme to make justice readily available in star chamber was surely that no account was taken of the human element: the persistence, stubbornness and chicanery of most litigants frustrated the cardinal's good intentions. Wolsey did not realise until too late that a policy which provided new facilities for litigants should not have failed to restrict the opportunities for abuse. The chancellor's answer to the growing number of plaintiffs who brought what were often trivial or frivolous suits before the council could then be no better than to delegate the task of adjudication to others. Disillusionment probably hit its peak on 19 April 1529. On this day, the 'sinister' suit of Joan Staunton for lands in Kidlington, Oxfordshire, was condemned as malicious and dismissed by a furious Wolsey.[39] The plaintiff had on several occasions summoned John Maunde and eleven co-defendants to London, where they had been obliged to appear in both star chamber and the white hall, despite the fact that there was 'at their commyng noo sufficient mattier laide ne objected again theim'. The suit was entirely frivolous: the plaintiff's pretended title was based on three 'peces of evidence, counterfetted and forged' by William Clerk of Burford. Wolsey promptly sent the forger to the Fleet and the false deeds were cut into pieces before the council. Sir Thomas Elyot, present in star chamber in his capacity as assistant to the clerk, described the incident and added comments of his own.[40] Why, he enquired, could not the law put a stop to the disruptions caused by the perpetual troublemakers who so vexed the cardinal and disturbed the council; why could not a system be devised which either contented such charlatans as Joan Staunton by the concession of a trifle, as a sop to Cerberus, or silenced them for ever under threat of rigorous penalties?

It was Elyot, however, not Wolsey, who was naive on this occasion. The Stauntons of the world were a constant nuisance and abused the council's facilities, but the cardinal was providing a public service by cancelling fake deeds and exposing forgers. Moreover, the most genuine plaintiffs who came into star chamber did so precisely because the contemporary law could not satisfactorily end civil disputes, especially those involving real property. The wider problems of litigation in the sixteenth century were multiplicity of suits in all the courts between parties, often substantially about the same matter; the use of procedural complexity as a means to frustrate valid claims; and the underdevelopment of existing legal doctrine, notably in forgery and fraud, perjury and the rules of evidence. Only in the council courts and chancery could early Tudor litigants and their advisers find a jurisdiction which was both competent and willing to tackle basic difficulties. Two examples will illustrate how the council in star chamber could go some way towards satisfying the needs of litigants harassed by unpleasant opponents.

George Blundell of Little Crosby, Lancashire, had in March 1513 been granted a life interest by his father, Nicholas Blundell, in the manor of Crosby and other lands in Little Crosby and Ditton.[41] The condition was that George should discharge his father's debts amounting to £130 out of the profits. George had only paid off one-third of this sum when he was disseised by Edward Molyneux, clerk, rector of Sefton. Molyneux claimed to have recovered the Blundell inheritance against Nicholas in an action on a writ of entry *sur disseisin in le post* before the justices of assize at Lancaster. Nicholas complained by bill to Sir Henry Marney, chancellor of the duchy; Molyneux replied with a suit against George, alleging that the latter had disseised his tenant. The dispute was referred to the justices at Lancaster in February 1516. Their report was received in the duchy chamber in Michaelmas term following, and Sir Henry decreed for the Blundells.[42] Molyneux therefore changed his approach: he returned to the duchy chamber and protested that no lease had ever been made by Nicholas to his son. He also pleaded that in an action of trespass at Preston sessions he had obtained a judgment directly contrary to the chancellor's. This was sufficient to re-open the suit before Sir Henry Marney, who ordered George Blundell to surrender possession.[43] Eventually the matter was referred again to the justices at Lancaster. Then old Nicholas Blundell died. George was not his father's heir: although his elder brother, Henry, had predeceased his father, Henry was succeeded by his son James. George retained an interest in the family inheritance by virtue of the lease of his sister-in-law's jointure; more pressing, however, were his father's creditors who remained two-thirds unsatisfied. George came into star chamber and made suit to Wolsey against Molyneux. The defendant's title was found to be bad and the cardinal pronounced a decree in the plaintiff's favour on 29 November 1524.[44] This provided that Molyneux should release the interest in the Blundell property which he had obtained by his 'recovery' at Lancaster, and that he should pay the outstanding debts of the deceased Nicholas on behalf of George. As the plaintiff had hoped, Wolsey decided that Molyneux, by interrupting George's possession and profits, had deprived the creditors of the repayment they would otherwise have received. Although the latter provision was unacceptable to Molyneux, it was eventually enforced upon him.[45] George Blundell succeeded in star chamber: Wolsey and the council recognised that his impending ruin was the result of his opponent's unjustified successes at Lancaster assizes and Preston sessions, compounded by the inability of the Blundells to get a definite result from the duchy chamber.

The second example, the suit of the Fleming family, reveals the willingness of the council to protect the rights of parties threatened with the obliteration of their title to land in the face of intransigence, chicanery and persistence on the part of their opponents. The suit concerned the manors of Credehoo, Puttesbrugh and Highbray in Devon, and first appeared in star chamber in 1490.[46] The plaintiff was then James Fleming, seventh lord Slane, and the defendants were Nicholas Dillon and Patrick Bellew. The title pleaded by the defendants was derived via their respective mothers Anne and Amy, sisters and co-heirs of the fourth lord Slane (*ob.* 1458).[47] The council, seeing right on both sides, put the dispute to arbitration, and an award was indented on 5 August 1490 which divided the lands equally between the parties.[48] By force of this settlement, James Fleming enjoyed two years' peaceful possession of his half of the land and was succeeded in title by his son Christopher, eighth lord Slane, who enjoyed possession for a further twenty-four years. Dillon and Bellew then seized the opportunity of Christopher's absence in Ireland to effect a recovery of his land by crafty pleading in an assize of *novel disseisin* – the defendant's appearance was not necessary in the assize[49] – and they obtained possession.[50] An anxious lord Slane complained to Wolsey in star chamber early in 1517, and on 20 February Dillon and Bellew were commanded by injunction to restore him to possession until their title had been examined, an order which both defendants entirely ignored. The cardinal referred the case once more to arbitrators, who were requested to determine the suit and to quieten all current actions between the parties 'aswell Reales as personales'.[51]

The arbitrators, who included Sir John Fineux and Robert Brudenell, decided that the award of 1490 was substantial and effective, having been indented with the consent of both sides, and resolved that it should stand as a final end between the parties for their mutual 'restfulness'.[52]

At this point, both Christopher Fleming and Nicholas Dillon died. The lady Elizabeth Fleming, Christopher's widow, promptly filed a bill of revivor, claiming the disputed land as her jointure.[53] Nicholas Dillon's title passed to his son Robert, who joined Bellew as co-defendant. The cardinal ordered writs of *subpoena* to be issued against the defendants, commanding their appearance in star chamber on 14 October 1518.[54] On that day Wolsey sat with a distinguished presence and a decree was pronounced.[55] The lady Elizabeth was to enjoy possession of her family's half of the three manors as awarded in 1490, in spite of the recovery in *novel disseisin*. Secondly, Bellew and the executors of Nicholas Dillon were to pay her £235 damages for loss of profits. In the event of 'slackness' in the execution of the decree, the sheriff of Devon was to intervene. On the following day, the council sat again: Bellew appeared before the presence and 'in playne corte Refused to obbey the saide decre'.[56] He was at once sent to the Tower by an angry cardinal. In addition process was awarded to the sheriff of Devon, authorising him to put lady Elizabeth in possession and to extend Bellew's lands, goods and chattels. If Bellew's friends resisted, the sheriff was to raise the *posse comitatus* and use force.[57] Bellew remained in the Tower for five and a half years.[58] Yet within months of obtaining her decree, lady Elizabeth – who had meanwhile married Thomas Dudley, Wolsey's servant – was back in star chamber. The sheriff of Devon had duly put her in possession and had removed Bellew's livestock for sale, but Bellew's son, Henry, had raised a following and rescued the animals from the sheriff's pound.[59]

How the cardinal reacted to this news is unknown. When the record resumes in 1526, lady Elizabeth was dead. With her departure, the Flemings were to come close to disinheritance. The position was that the eighth lord Slane had made a settlement of his estate in 1505, executing a feoffment to the use of himself and his legitimate issue, while retaining possession and providing a jointure for his wife by arrangement with the feoffees.[60] After lady Elizabeth's death, the feoffees succeeded her in possession: the young James Fleming was in his nonage and resided in Ireland. The latter circumstances presented Bellew and Robert Dillon with a golden opportunity. Since the disputed land was held by knight service, the enfeoffment to uses had not deprived the king of his wardship.[61] The two claimants sued a *monstrans de droit* in chancery, and in 1529 obtained judgment for possession by *ouster le main* after pleading their recovery in *novel disseisin*.[62] They were restored to possession by the escheator and, when ousted, began an action of entry in the nature of an assize against the feoffees in the court of common pleas.[63] Success seemed assured: the feoffees had their price and were persuaded to fail in their appearance in common pleas. The demandants then moved the court to a judgment by default, which was possible in this action without trial of the principal charge.[64] The judges had queries, however, and held back. The delay was sufficient for news of the action to reach James and a bill of complaint was at once filed in star chamber.[65] Bellew (by then aged seventy) and Robert Dillon were summoned to appear before the council, and on 22 November 1531 were examined as to the circumstances of their action in common pleas.[66] It is a disappointment that the later progress of the suit cannot be brought to light. There can be little doubt that Sir Thomas More would have protected the Fleming interest against obliteration by demandants who were in combination with dishonest feoffees. Bellew died in September 1533 and the next generation of claimants may have let his persistence die with him.[67] From the later evidence which can be found,[68] it appears that the council in star chamber had succeeded in defeating the threat to the Fleming family's right and in maintaining the integrity of the settlement indented in 1490.

The impact of the council's justice under Wolsey should be viewed in the context of the English judicial system as a whole. The cardinal appreciated the demand in his day for the more

general availability of facilities for litigation based on the conciliar tradition of equitable proceedings. He had gained early
practical experience of the requirements of litigants as a junior
councillor in attendance at the royal court.[69] The early Tudor
legal landscape was distinguished not by conflicting legal
theory but by shifting areas of jurisdiction: the courts of king's
bench and common pleas were losing business; the courts of
the council and chancery were gaining it.[70] This is not the old
canard about Roman law. Dr Ives has explained that little
danger existed of the reception of substantive Roman law into
England, and at no point did Wolsey aim to transform the
courts over which he presided into civil law courts.[71] This is
confirmed by the action taken against Dr Stokesley in January
1523.[72] The shift marked, rather, the rise of an alternative
system of courts based on the council and chancery. The cardinal took the point and encouraged the trend. Naturally he
had his critics – serious as well as scurrilous – and Wolsey's
own thoughtlessness and self-aggrandisement justified many of
the accusations against him.[73] A positive side to the account is,
however, firmly established by the extent to which the cardinal
secured the active co-operation of the common-law judges,
sergeants-at-law and counsellors-at-the-bar in the service of
the council and chancery.[74] Sir Richard Broke was
particularly energetic, and even Sir John Fineux and Sir
Anthony Fitzherbert, who both had reason to hate the cardinal
and all his works, were regular in their advice and assistance.
Eventually the common lawyers succeeded in remedying many
of the defects in their system – but this was for the future. It
was Wolsey, for all his faults, who emphasised the chancellor's
wider role, perceiving that a strong conciliar jurisdiction had
the potential to resolve conflict and confusion and to overthrow
self-help and chicanery. The high court of star chamber was
essentially his achievement.

THE COURT OF STAR CHAMBER

On 19 October 1529, the day after the cardinal's fall from office, the council met under the presidency of the duke of Norfolk to debate the succession to Wolsey. The discussion was adjourned and then resumed four days later at Greenwich, when the king himself presided.[75] Opinion turned on the choice of a layman and, after some hesitation, Sir Thomas More took the chancellor's oath in Westminster hall on 26 October.[76] More was undoubtedly the best-qualified candidate for the position: a skilled lawyer and a former chancellor of the duchy, a former king's secretary and diplomat. As a result of his opposition to the royal divorce, however, his chancellorship was to develop into a struggle for the king's favour and political power.[77] Before long three conflicting policies were simultaneously represented at the council board, in parliament and at the royal court. At the opening of the 1529 session of parliament, the author of *Utopia* had announced his own plan for the reform of the realm by the enactment of laws in restraint of 'new enormities . . . amongst the people'.[78] More also aimed to defend the church from attacks which were in part the direct result of Wolsey's neglect of its affairs.[79] During 1531 Thomas Cromwell proposed his rival design for the more radical reformation of state and church and the reconstruction of the commonwealth.[80] Lastly, there remained the conservative standpoint of the lay aristocracy as vested in the dukes of Norfolk and Suffolk – hardly a 'policy' but a major political force. After the departure of the cardinal, the unreformed king's council was to fulfil with a vengeance its traditional role as a vehicle for consultation, participation and the satisfaction of individual ambition.

As chancellor, More's declared purpose was the suppression of 'enormities', and as a first step to that end the so-called act '*pro camera stellata*' was revived in 1529.[81] The new statute recited the tenor of the old, with its emphasis on the need for ministerial jurisdiction to combat perversions of public justice, and appointed the president of the council as a judge of the tribunal created by the earlier act, alongside the chancellor, treasurer and keeper of the privy seal. As its form indicated, the 1529 act had a dual function. It reconstituted the 1487 tribunal, which subsequently met and is known to have inquired into allegations of misdemeanour,[82] though the evidence is insufficient either to establish the location and frequency of its sessions, or to illuminate its relationship (if any) with the council in star chamber. The other intention behind the enactment was to give high official rank to the duke of Suffolk. Charles Brandon, fourth duke of Suffolk and the king's brother-in-law, had for years been outshone by Wolsey, and there was talk in October 1529 that his ambition to succeed the cardinal as chancellor was only thwarted by the opposition of the duke of Norfolk.[83] The French ambassador was right when he assessed the order of precedence in the council as first Norfolk then Suffolk,[84] but the latter did not hold major office, a circumstance which – as the act of 1529 observed in its second, rarely printed section – had excluded him, under Wolsey, from attending such important events as the swearing-in of sheriffs and justices of the peace, and the fixing of wine prices.[85] Suffolk was therefore appointed president of the council, an office which had lapsed after the death of Henry VII but to which the 1529 statute gave high status, and was observed by the Spanish ambassador as acting in that role 'with the same authority as the chancellor' for the purpose of assisting the king when Norfolk and Sir Thomas More were absent.[86] For unexplained reasons, however, the revival of the ministerial tribunal as an official agency of inquiry into the prevalence of misdemeanour in the realm was short-lived. By the end of 1530, Suffolk's office had returned to the obscurity from which it had suddenly emerged.[87]

In terms of the implementation of positive reform, More had realised by 1531 that he was in a false position.[88] The divorce and the attempt to break the spirit of the clergy in convocation had taken priority over all other subjects in the minds of the king's advisers. More was unable to participate in either debate, and his influence on the government's policy was soon eroded. The political crisis was, however, insufficient to disrupt the regular work of the council courts. When the council had met on 19 October 1529, it had resolved that 'there shalbe sittinge in this Court for hearing and expedicion of all maner Causes here dependinge, Tewsdaie, Thursedaie and Satterdaye'.[89] The decision did not preclude the council from dealing with suits on an *ad hoc* basis at other meetings if time permitted. What it did, rather, was to recognise the irreversible reality that Wolsey's policy had transformed 'star chamber' into a settled court of the realm. There was no decline in the volume of litigation in star chamber after the cardinal's disgrace: litigation was maintained in all the courts of equitable proceedings at the level established in the later years of his supremacy. Under Sir Thomas More, it was precisely the chancellor's increasing political isolation which enabled him to devote so much of his time to matters of justice.[90] About a hundred and twenty suits a year were in progress at the various procedural stages in star chamber throughout the 1530s, a rate of business which not only strengthened the position of conciliar jurisdiction as a rival to that of the courts of common law, but also supported continuing awareness of the problems which had moved the cardinal to consider the reform of the council in 1525/6.

By his conduct in star chamber, More justified his reputation as a sagacious judge, critical but fair, his only failing being the tendency to indulge his sardonic humour where Wolsey would have preferred straightforward impatience.[91] His special contribution to his courts of chancery and the council came in the field of the better enforcement of final decrees. Under Wolsey, the council had gone some way towards combating the failure of unsuccessful parties to obey its decrees in civil suits, and the point was clearly crucial to the success of star chamber as a central court for private litigation. Although penal recognisances might still be employed in all circumstances after 1529, More tended to prefer the enforcement of decrees for the recovery of real or personal property by injunction.[92] An innovation was the imposition of the threat of double damages for non-compliance.[93] In the face of direct disobedience, More streamlined the method sometimes invoked under Wolsey by which 'special' writs of execution were addressed to the sheriff of the county, commanding him to enforce the council's order – using force if necessary – and to bind those who opposed him to 'good abearing' or to their appearance before the council.[94] The chancellor's attitude to enforcement gave substance to the concept of finality in conciliar decrees. Wolsey had often been tentative, sometimes even irresolute, perhaps hoping that parties would ultimately agree to settle their differences in a spirit of equitable compromise. More applied the relative severity of common law doctrine to the theory of the 'final end' – needless to say his approach was an obvious attraction to plaintiffs seeking redress against obdurate defendants.

Politics did not therefore restrict the development of star chamber as a court in the early 1530s, but the quest for the royal divorce and the struggle for power had an effect on the composition and structure of the council, and its relationship with star chamber. With the rise of Cromwell's influence at court in the autumn of 1531, the political scene quickly veered away from Westminster. By 1532 a situation had emerged which was not dissimilar to that which had existed from 1509-15: an 'inner ring' of leading councillors, managed by Cromwell, had assumed the advisory and executive duties of the old council attendant.[95] More held out to the end, only resigning the chancellorship on 16 May 1532, the day after the clergy's final Submission.[96] The situation then remained fairly constant until March 1533, when Cromwell's Act in Restraint of Appeals heralded the break with Rome and the triumph of the radical policy.[97] The ascendancy of a council attendant could no longer upset the routine of star chamber or chancery:[98] it was no coincidence that the new keeper of the great seal, Sir Thomas Audley, was not a member of the 'inner ring'. Cromwell's correspondent, writing from London, could thus assure him late in 1532 that Audley and the others of the central council continued to sit daily in the *camera stellata*, 'by which means all is in good order here'.[99] Undoubtedly, however, the division of conciliar activity between 1531 and 1533 brought about a degree of differentiation in the conciliar function some three years ahead of Cromwell's specific act of reconstruction. Differentiation received overt recognition by the appointment in January 1533 of Thomas Derby as 'Clarke of our Counsaill attending uppon our person', the office which by March 1538 was established as the clerkship of Cromwell's privy council.[100] The bias of the council's advisory and executive aspect had removed to the royal court. Derby's exact status remains mysterious, but his work was definitely not in matters of justice. Sir William Sulyard, one of those nominated to the bench at the white hall in Hilary term 1529, had already been summoned to join the council attendant to undertake the hearing of 'poor men's causes'.[101]

The tendency towards differentiation in the council was, nevertheless, incapable of splitting it into its component parts. Institutional fluidity prevailed until 1536, when the bifurcation of the Henrician king's council into the new privy council and the court of star chamber was achieved by Cromwell's fundamental reform of the system.[102] The prime feature of the reconstruction, from the court's point of view, was that it gave star chamber the professionalism and continuity that could only stem from a settled constitution. The privy council and the court of star chamber were distinct in every way, but they had almost the same membership. The selection of privy councillors had not left the residue of former councillors in the court. Those men who were not important or active enough to reach the privy council were excluded also from star chamber, retaining only a ceremonial status during their lifetimes as 'councillors at large'. The institutional organisation of the privy council was complete when it met on 10 August 1540 – eighteen days after Cromwell's execution – to appoint a clerk and inaugurate a minute book.[103] The same may be said of star chamber. The extant lists of attendances in the court verify its final establishment by 1540. The 'high court of star chamber', as it styled itself in its decrees, comprised the members of the privy council plus the legal experts, the chief or (sometimes) puisne justices and the chief baron of the exchequer.[104]

As Elton reminds us, it was the privy council, not the star

chamber, which was deliberately created: the court simply carried on – in business, place and time of meetings, and institutional character – where the old council left off. [105] On the other hand, Cromwell certainly envisaged the fully-fledged court. The abortive plans which he sketched out late in 1533 had illuminated the direction of his thoughts. [106] They revealed his confidence in star chamber's future as an impartial criminal court, by proposing an act authorising the trial there of murders committed in Wales and the marches. [107] They also suggested that Cromwell, interestingly enough, was eager to confuse the enforcement role of the ministerial tribunals of the Lancastrian period, 1487, and 1529 with the court of star chamber. A second idea was to make an act enabling the lord chancellor and two judges to proceed in all cases in star chamber, despite the absence of the other officers demanded by the statutes. This was 'for speed of justice to the king's subjects'. [108] Perhaps, as a former pupil of Wolsey, Cromwell could justifiably regard the distinction as somewhat academic. Later plans and 'remembrances' made it clear that Cromwell approved the continuation of star chamber's supervisory and homiletic role over those concerned with administration and justice in the realm. [109] Although official prosecutions were still few in the later 1530s, the court steadily fortified the position held by the cardinal against corruption, malfeasance and the perversion of justice by sheriffs, justices of the peace, jurors and others. [110] Similarly, the 'orations' delivered by Wolsey in star chamber to the justices of the peace were repeated by Audley and Cromwell. [111] The investigatory and police jurisdiction previously enjoyed by the Henrician council passed after 1536 to the new privy council, but a general supervisory function over legal machinery remained inherent in star chamber. It was not long before the court had acquired stature as a deterrent to judicial corruption and abuse, so that men could declare how it was 'a greater Terror to the Country to abyde the Judgement of the Starre chambre' than to suffer other forms of inquiry. [112]

Cromwell in addition gave energetic support to star chamber's function as a popular court for civil litigation within

the areas of business established under Henry VII and Wolsey.
The records confirm that the new minister shared the cardinal's concern for the provision of more and better justice,
and that he was prepared to allow the progressive development
of the rival system of courts based on the council and chancery.
Unlike Wolsey, however, Cromwell was not content to unload
the brunt of the work upon others, although star chamber continued to accede willingly to requests for the appointment of
commissioners to end suits in the localities. As far as can be
discovered, Cromwell was almost as active in the court as he
was in the privy council, and he employed his servants in tasks
of arbitration and compromise.[113] He was not lord chancellor
but he was the motive force behind the conciliar courts.
Cromwell's contemporaries were aware that he spent a great
amount of time in dealing with the complaints of the people
and on endeavours to satisfy the public demand for justice.[114]
The same consideration produced his bureaucratic reforms in
the chancery (as master of the rolls) and in part underlay his
planning of financial courts.[115] His enterprise was also
responsible for the transformation of the group of councillors
in the white hall into the court of requests.[116] The change was
admittedly necessitated by the reconstruction of the council,
but Cromwell kept in touch with the bench in the white hall
and sent instructions to the masters of requests.[117]

Decades of work by lord chancellors, privy councillors,
judges and practising lawyers were required before the court of
star chamber reached the height of its maturity. By the time
that Sir Thomas Egerton became Elizabeth I's last lord
keeper in 1596, the court had long ceased to try titles. While
many suits remained which were related to litigation elsewhere
over real or personal property, the court had primarily become
a central criminal court concerned with the making and interpretation of legal doctrine and the enforcement of common and
statute law. The extant star chamber *Reports* testify to the
court's vitality as an institution and to its supreme but integral
position in the English judicial system.[118] The authority of the
court penetrated to all levels of judicial practice. As Sir
Edward Coke explained, 'this court [is] as well for Instruction

as correction'.[119] Much was, however, owed to star chamber's early life and direction. Without the vision and originality of Thomas Wolsey, despite the better practical abilities of his successors, the council in star chamber would not have realised its full potential. Sir Thomas Smith shall have the last word:

> This court began long before, but tooke great augmentation and authoritie at that time that Cardinall *Wolsey* Archbishop of Yorke was Chauncellor of Englande, who of some was thought to have first devised the Court, because that he after some intermission by negligence of time, augmented the authoritie of it ... Sith that time this court hath beene in more estimation, and is continued to this day.[120]

Notes

CHAPTER 1

1. See J. A. Guy, 'Wolsey's Star Chamber: a study in archival reconstruction', *Journal of the Society of Archivists,* v (April 1975), 169–80.
2. *Ibid.,* pp.174–80. The Henrician council registers contained everything of importance to the historian of the early Tudor court which is not now among the court's extant records in the P.R.O. Until the reign of Elizabeth, virtually the whole of star chamber's activity was recorded in these volumes: interlocutory orders and final decrees, orders for writs of *subpoena* or privy seal summonses, orders for commissions of *dedimus potestatem,* entries of appearances, admissions to attorney, rules upon consent, and affidavits.
3. E.g. M. McKisack, *Medieval History in the Tudor Age* (Oxford, 1971), 75–94.
4. The confusion between the court of star chamber and the statute 3 Hen. VII, c.1 was in full swing by 1565; Bayne, pp.1xviii-xx.
5. E1 2768, fos. 57–8.
6. *Ibid.,* fo. 57.
7. *Ibid.*
8. *Ibid.*
9. *Ibid.,* fo. 57v. (interlineation).
10. *Ibid.,* fo. 57v.

11 On Mill's succession to the clerkship, Hargrave 216, fos. 104v., 127v.

12 Hargrave 216, fos.104v.–19v.; Additional 4521, fos.64–103v.; Additional 26,647, fos.204–15; C.U.L. Additional MS. 3105, fos.90–128; Corpus Christi College, Oxford, MS. 196, pp.75–115; Bodleian MS. Eng. hist. c. 304, fos.265–300. C.U.L. Additional MS. 3105 is dated 'Anno domini 1590 et Tricesimo secundo Elizabethae Regine' (fo.90). Cf. Elfreda Skelton, 'The Court of Star Chamber in the Reign of Queen Elizabeth', University of London M.A. thesis (1931), Pt. 1, pp.14–15. I am grateful to Lady Neale for permission to refer to her thesis.

13 C.U.L. Additional MS. 3105, fo.90v. The attorneys claimed that the clerk aimed to draw them to Gray's Inn to 'sit and wait' there as his underclerks, while extorting the moiety of their fees for copying the current records. Cf. E1 2669, 2680.

14 Ibid., fo.93v.

15 The remains of Mill's researches are to be found in E1 2768, passim; Hargrave 216, fos.100–4v., 119v.–83v.

16 C.U.L. Additional MS. 3105, fo.99.

17 Ibid., fos.99v.–100.

18 E1 2768, fo.1.

19 C. L. Scofield, A Study of the Court of Star Chamber (Chicago, 1900), 40–1.

20 Additional 24,926; Additional 4521, fos.35–64; Corpus Christi College, Oxford, MS. 196, pp.47–74; Bodleian MS. Eng. hist. c. 304, fos.238–65; All Souls College MS. 178a, fos.64–86. This version is printed in A Collection of Curious Discourses written by Eminent Antiquaries upon Several Heads in our English Antiquities, ed. Thomas Hearne, ii, no.38, where it is wrongly attributed to Francis Tate. Additional 24,926 is dated 20 March 1585/86; Additional 4521 at fo.35 is stated to be by Lambarde, as are the remaining mss. Cf. Skelton, pp.8–10; Scofield, Study of Star Chamber, pp.81–2; Archeion or a Discourse upon the High Courts of Justice in England, ed. C. H. McIlwain and P. L. Ward (Cambridge, Mass. 1957), 160.

21 Folger Shakespeare Library, Washington D.C., MS. 511121.1. This ms. is Lambarde's own copy, and carries his marginal notes and interlinear changes. Lambarde's autograph appears twice, and the ms. is dated 1589 in his hand. In view of the survival of the author's copy, the citing of references to other mss. is unnecessary. This version was incorporated into the 1591 Archeion, which was presented to Sir Robert Cecil in the autumn of that year.

22 *Ibid.*, fo.31v.

23 Hargrave 216, fos.109v.–10, 116.

24 Folger MS. 511121.1, fo.28v.

25 *Ibid.*, fo.33.

26 *Infra* p. 20.

27 Lambarde's argument is set out in Folger MS. 511121.1, fos.31v.–38v. Whereas, for example, before 1487 the king's council sitting as a court allowed only such plaintiffs to proceed by bill of complaint as showed willingness to stand to the jurisdiction of the court, either by binding themselves to prove their suits or by producing pledges of the prosecution, after 1487 the ministers mentioned in the act enjoyed statutory powers to command enforcement of their decisions.

28 21 Hen. VIII, c.20; *infra* p.132–3.

29 On the acceptance of this interpretation, see Bayne, pp.lxx–xxii. Cf. Sir William Holdsworth, *A History of English Law,* i. (rev. ed., London, 1956), 492–5.

30 Mss. of Hudson's treatise are relatively common. Those at the B.M. are Lansdowne 622; Harleian 736, 1226, 1689, 4274, 6235, 6256; Hargrave 251, 290, 291; Stowe 419; Additional 11,681, 26,647. It is evident that soon after its composition Hudson's treatise enjoyed a fairly wide circulation in manuscript; in the absence of the author's original, it is generally agreed that the most reliable version available is Harleian 1226. This copy contains the well-known memorandum by Sir John Finch: 'This Treatise was compiled by William Hudson of Grais Inne Esq[r] one very much practized and of great experience in the Starrchamber: and my very affectionate friend. His sonne and heyr M[r] Christopher Hudson (whose handwryting this booke is) after his fathers death gave it to mee. 19[0] Decembris, 1635 Jo: Finch' (fo.2v.). I remain unconvinced that this memorandum is not a copy; it also appears in Additional 11,681, which ms. also has a strong claim to authenticity. The copy of the treatise subsequently referred to (G. R. Elton's ms.) is an excellent one, directly related to Additional 11,681. The treatise was printed, very badly, by Francis Hargrave in *Collectanea Juridica,* ii (1792), 1–240. Hargrave's text was based on a collation of two mss., and of these one was inaccurate and the other incomplete (*ibid.*, p.239).

31 A memorandum by John Lightfoot recorded that Hudson presented his treatise 'to the Lord BP of Lincolne at his first com-

eing to the Seale for whose use it was originally prepared and digested into that Method'; Lansdowne 639, fo.99v. If the treatise was composed in the period after the last precedent among Hudson's notes as they survive in Lansdowne 639 and before the presentation to bishop Williams, the original version of the work may be confidently assigned to the years 1618 to 1621. Lightfoot's testimony is confirmed by a dedicatory note which introduces the handsome though incomplete copy of the treatise now at the Huntington Library (E1 7921). There J[ohn] E[vans], senior examiner in the court of star chamber in the 1620s, recorded that the book was first written by Hudson and then presented by him to Williams on his accession to the great seal. Certainly, the original treatise pre-dated July 1621. However, internal evidence establishes that the version of the work which we now have dates from the early years of the reign of Charles I. It seems that Hudson then expanded the original text.

32 Hudson, fo.11v.; *Coll. Jur.*, ii.10.

33 *Ibid.*, fo.57v.; *Coll. Jur.*, ii.50.

34 This was a reference to Henry II's ordinance of 1178. Cf. *Select Charters*, ed. W. Stubbs (9th ed., rev. by H. W. C. Davis, Oxford, 1921), 155.

35 Hudson, fo.26; *Coll. Jur.*, ii.22–3.

36 *Ibid.*, fo.27; *Coll. Jur.*, ii.23–4.

37 *Ibid.*, fos.41v.–42; *Coll. Jur.*, ii.36.

38 *Ibid.*, fos.59v.–61; *Coll. Jur.*, ii.52–5.

39 Scofield, *Study of Star Chamber*, 55.

40 Hudson, fos.62v.–63; *Coll. Jur.*, ii.55.

41 *Ibid.*, fo.179v.; *Coll. Jur.*, ii.168. Isaac Cotton's treatise is useful for comparative purposes. It was entitled 'The Course and manner of prosecucon of Causes in the highe Court of Starchamber from the originall Subpoena unto the hearing and end of the Cause'. The best copy is Lansdowne 639, fos.1–21v. The treatise was complete in 1622; cf. Skelton, p.16.

42 The standard authorities are J. F. Baldwin, *The King's Council in England during the Middle Ages* (Oxford, 1913); *Select Cases before the King's Council, 1243–1482*, ed. I. S. Leadam and J. F. Baldwin (Selden Society, xxxv, 1918); 'The King's Council', by J. F. Baldwin, and 'The Chancery', by B. Wilkinson, in *The English Government at Work, 1327–1336*, ed. J. F. Willard and W. A. Morris, i. (Cambridge, Mass., 1940), 129–205.

43 The reference of 9 May 1392 is in C44/37B.

44 Leadam and Baldwin, p.xvi.

45 *Ibid.*

46 *Ibid.*

47 *Ibid.*, p.xvii; cf. Sir, J. Fortescue, *The Governance of England,* ed. C. Plummer (Oxford, 1885), 148.

48 A. Harding, *The Law Courts of Medieval England* (London, 1973), 99–100.

49 Baldwin, *King's Council,* pp.247–9; Leadam and Baldwin, p.xxiii.

50 *Ibid.;* Wilkinson, 'The Chancery', p.193.

51 Wilkinson, 'The Chancery', p.194.

52 Cf. the introductory note to the C 256 class list at the P.R.O. by Dr Patricia Barnes; C 256/2/4 no. 1; C 256/3/1 nos. 7, 20; C 256/3/4 no. 8; C 256/3/5 no. 5; C 256/4/1 no. 9; C 256/4/2 nos. 1B, 17; C 256/6/1 no. 8; C 256/6/2 no. 35. Baldwin, *King's Council,* pp.265–76.

53 C 44/1/3; Wilkinson, 'The Chancery', pp.194–5.

54 Leadam and Baldwin, pp.xxiii–iv, 76–7; Baldwin, *King's Council,* pp.251–2.

55 Baldwin, *King's Council,* pp.147–208; N. Pronay, 'The Chancellor, the Chancery, and the Council at the end of the fifteenth century', *British Government and Administration,* ed. H. Hearder and H. R. Loyn (Cardiff, 1974), 87.

56 This development can be traced in the early *subpoena* files, C 253/1–52; cf. the introductory note to the C 253 class list at the P.R.O. by Dr Barnes.

57 Leadam and Baldwin, pp.xxvii–xxx; Harding, pp.103–5.

58 Harding, pp.105–7, 184–8.

59 E.g. E 28/93, 96, *passim; Select Cases before the King's Council in the Star Chamber . . . A.D. 1477–1509,* ed. I. S. Leadam (Selden Society, xvi, 1903), 1–15.

60 Pronay, p.98. This was, of course, the great advantage enjoyed by the mature court of star chamber.

61 The best discussion is Pronay, pp.96–101.

62 Baldwin, *King's Council,* pp.429–34 and references cited there.

63 J. R. Lander, 'Council, Administration and Councillors, 1461 to 1485', *Bulletin of the Institute of Historical Research,* xxxii (1959), 164–5, 179–80.

64 *Ibid.,* p.165 no.2.

65 S. B. Chrimes, *Henry VII* (London, 1972), 100–101.

66 *Ibid.,* p.151.

67 Bayne, pp.xix–xxii.

68 *Ibid.*, p.xlviii.

69 *Ibid.*

70 Bayne, pp.xxix–xxxvi.

71 Lander, pp.152–3.

72 Chrimes, *Henry VII,* p.103.

73 Cf. Lander, p.156; Chrimes, *Henry VII,* ch. 4 especially pp.101–14.

74 Chrimes, *Henry VII,* p.103.

75 E1 2652, fo.3v.

76 *Ibid.*; cf. the introductory discussion in J. A. Guy, 'A Conciliar Court of Audit at work in the last months of the reign of Henry VII', *B.I.H.R.,* xlix (1976), 289–95.

77 Bayne, pp.xviii–ix.

78 E1 2652, fos.1–8.

79 *Ibid.*

80 *Ibid.*, fo.1v.; cf. Bayne, pp.8, 58.

81 Bayne, pp.xviii–ix.

82 E1 2652, fo.1v.

83 Bayne, p.xix.

84 *Ibid.*, p.13.

85 *Ibid.*

86 E1 2652, fo.1v.

87 Bayne, p.8.

88 E1 2652, fos.1–8; Bayne, pp.1–15.

89 Bayne, pp.9–59; E1 2652, *passim.*

90 Reynold Bray, chancellor of the duchy and member of the council learned (died 1503).

91 Thomas Lovell, chancellor of the exchequer and treasurer of the chamber (to 1492).

92 John Morton, lord chancellor and archbishop of Canterbury (died 1500).

93 Richard Fox, keeper of the privy seal (1487–1516), bishop of Exeter (1487–92), Bath (to 1494), Durham (to 1501) and Winchester (died 1528).

94 Bayne, pp.xl–vii; Chrimes, *Henry VII,* pp.149–52; R. Somerville, 'Henry VII's "Council Learned in the Law" ', *E.H.R.,* liv (1939), 427–42; Guy, 'A Conciliar Court of Audit', pp.289–95.

95 G. R. Elton, 'Tudor Government: the points of contact – the Council', *Transactions of the Royal Historical Society,* 5th series, xxv (1975), 200–201.

 96 On the problem of security generally, Chrimes, *Henry VII*, ch. 3.
 97 Chrimes, *Henry VII*, p.98.
 98 E.g. Bayne, pp.13, 29–30.
 99 Articles cited at n. 94 *supra*.
100 Bayne, p.xix; E1 2652, fo.1v.; REQ 1/1, fo.1.
101 *Ibid.*
102 Bayne, pp.xxxvi–vii, 54–8.
103 *Ibid.*, pp.xxxvii–xl; endorsements on proceedings in unsorted
     bundles REQ 3/3–6.
104 REQ 1/1, fo.82. His office provided the essential qualifications
     for the appointment, since he commanded a secretarial service
     and could compel appearances before the council, swiftly if
     necessary, by privy seal summons. Fox was, however, replaced in
     1495 by Thomas Savage, then bishop of Rochester, who subse-
     quently sat 'lord presedent of the Kyng['s] counsayle chambur'
     on progress, until he himself was superseded in 1502 by Richard
     Fitzjames, then also bishop of Rochester. Edmund Dudley
     appears to have held the office of president of the council from
     1506–9, though undoubtedly for a purpose other than justice. As
     Fox's successors had no ready access to a seal, they were
     authorised to instruct the clerks of the signet to compose
     documents at court which served as writs of summons, com-
     missions, orders and the like. These were sealed with the signet
     seal by the king's secretary, who also resided in the household,
     and were known as 'letters missive'. The king's sign manual was
     often provided but, for practical reasons, was equally often
     omitted. Cf. Bayne, pp.xxxvii–xl; Historical Manuscripts Com-
     mission, *Various Collections*, ii. (London, 1903), 31–8; en-
     dorsements on proceedings, and signet letters in unsorted
     bundles REQ 3/3–6.
105 REQ 1/1, fos.79–83.
106 *Select Cases in the Court of Requests*, ed. I. S. Leadam (Selden Socie-
     ty, xii, 1898), cii–ix; endorsements on proceedings in unsorted
     bundles REQ 3/3–6. Chrimes, *Henry VII*, p.153.
107 *Ibid.*
108 *Ibid.*
109 E1 2652, fo.2v.; *Calendar of Patent Rolls, 1476–1485*, 413, 497, 538.
110 The lords of the council in *camera stellata* were beginning to be
     regarded as a court in the reign of Henry VII; Bayne, p.lxxv;
     2/5/128, 18/41.
111 2/31/142.

112 Especially Bayne, pp.11, 13–16, 18, 21–2, 28–30, 35, 42.

113 *The Paston Letters,* ed. J. Gairdner (London, 1895), iii. 385.

114 Bayne, pp.cxi–lxv.

115 In particular 5 Edw. III, c.9; 25 Edw. III, St. 5, c.4; 28 Edw. III, c.3.

116 On these problems the statute 32 Hen. VIII, c.9 is instructive.

117 E.g. the correct identification of those to be indicted or the clarification of contradictory evidence; Bayne, pp.11, 22, 28; E1 2652, fo.4v.

118 E.g. Bayne, pp.cli–ii, 84–5; 2/19/63, 27/84; E1 2652, fos.4v., 6.

119 Bayne, p.7; on treason considered by the council, *ibid.,* p.32.

120 *Infra,* p.65.

121 Bayne, pp.cxxix–xlviii, cliii–iv.

122 *Ibid.,* pp.cxxix–xxxv.

123 The additional documents are now mainly scattered through the unlisted bundles of STAC 10, and amongst the folders of unlisted papers and fragments in the later boxes of STAC 2.

124 This figure allows also for suits known only from the Ellesmere extracts. It must still, however, be an underestimate.

125 *Infra,* p.18; *pace* Chrimes, *Henry VII,* p.147.

126 Bayne, pp.cxi–lxv.

127 *Ibid.,* pp.cxxxvii–ix.

128 *Ibid.,* pp.cxxxvi–vii, 129.

129 *Ibid.,* p.cxxxix.

130 *Ibid.,* pp.cliv–lxv; E1 2652, fos.1, 9.

131 Bayne, pp.cliv–lxv, 30; E1 2652, fos.10–11.

132 2/31/142.

132 2/31/142.

133 E1 2652, fos.1, 9; Bayne, pp.14, 25–6.

134 E1 2652, fo.9; F. Blomefield, *History of the County of Norfolk,* ii (London, 1805), 449.

135 Bayne, p.23; E1 2652, fo.1v.

136 Bayne, p.25.

137 E1 2652, fo.9.

138 Bayne, p.25.

139 *Ibid.;* E1 2652, fo.2v.

140 Bayne, p.46.

141 *Ibid.,* pp.cxi–liv. The assessment takes into account the record material unknown to Bayne, and also the Ellesmere extracts.

142 In this paragraph I am indebted to the paper read to the Cambridge Legal History Conference on 9 July 1975 by DeLloyd J.

Guth. I am very grateful to Dr Guth for sending me a transcript of his paper.

143 E.g. 13 Hen. IV, c.7; 2 Hen. V, St. 1, c.8; 11 Hen. VII, c.7. Leadam, *Star Chamber 1477–1509*, pp.234–37.

144 Bayne, pp.cxxxix–cl, 22, 25, 41–4; Leadam, *Star Chamber 1477–1509*, pp.237–53. Note, however, that a conviction for riot might be obtained though nothing was done 'but by words and bearinge of weapons'; Bayne, p.46.

145 Bayne, pp.cxii–xiv.

146 *Ibid.*, pp.cxix, 17.

147 *Ibid.*, pp.cxxvii–ix.

148 *Ibid.*, pp.cl, c–cii.

149 *Ibid.*, p.cl.

150 *Ibid.*, p.cliii.

151 *Ibid.*, p.cl.

152 *Ibid.*, p.cliii.

153 *Ibid.*, pp.cxlviii–ix, 20.

154 *Ibid.*, pp.cli–ii; Leadam, *Star Chamber 1477–1509*, pp.cxii–xiii, 130–7.

155 Bayne, pp.20, 33; 2/26/11. The fourth case is *Attorney-general* v. *Brandesby et al.*, 2/2/164, 165, 204, 209, 20/27, 22/134, 286. Bayne (p.cxxxi) believed that this prosecution was not taken in star chamber but before the tribunal established by 3 Hen. VII, c.1; unfortunately, the probabilities are all the other way, since the examinations were without exception taken down by Robert Rydon, the clerk of the council in star chamber.

156 *Attorney-general* v. *Hall et al.*, in Bayne, p.33.

157 E.g. 2/2/164, 165, 204, 209.

158 Bayne, p.33.

159 2/26/11; the case also occurs fortuitously in the Ellesmere extracts, Bayne, pp.20, 22.

160 Bayne, p.20.

161 2/26/11.

162 As it could well have been. A. Conway, *Henry VII's Relations with Scotland and Ireland, 1485–1498* (Cambridge, 1932), 1–26.

163 Bayne, p.lxi.

164 *Ibid.*, pp.xlix–lxiv.

165 *Ibid.*, p.60.

166 Pronay, p.99.

167 Bayne, pp.60–1.

168 *Ibid.*, pp.liv–viii, lxiv–xviii, 27–8, 61–73, and references cited.

169 This is clear from the clerical endorsements on the proceedings, which are in a form, script and position peculiar to chancery and quite distinct from the endorsement made by the clerk of the council on a star chamber bill; cf. T. G. Barnes, *Speculum*, xxxiv (1959), 650–1.

170 Cf. Pronay, pp.99–100.

171 Pronay, p.99; Bayne, pp.cxvi–vii.

172 Bayne, pp.28–9.

173 11 Hen. VII, c.25. The master of the rolls was no doubt added because the act extended to perjury committed in chancery and before the council. Not only did this officer have custody of the chancery records, the files still including many documents concerning proceedings before the council, he was also experienced in conducting the examinations of defendants and witnesses according to the procedure of the council and chancery, and was well qualified to detect perjury in proceedings before the special court itself.

174 Bayne, pp.lxii–xiii.

CHAPTER 2

1 Lord Herbert of Cherbury, *The Life and Reign of King Henry the Eighth* (London, 1672), 2–3.

2 See, for example, the countersignatures in C 82/335, 338, 341, 355, 364, 365, 374; B.M. Additional 6,214, fo.4; Lansdowne 1, fo.140.

3 Lord Herbert, *Henry the Eighth*, p.3.

4 E1 2655, fos.7–9v.; Lansdowne 639, fos.27, 28, 33, 34v., 40v., 44v., 45.

5 It became the accepted rule under Warham that the council could not sit in the absence of the lord chancellor; Lansdowne 639, fo.40v.

6 This is the impression given by the Ellesmere extracts; Bayne, pp.44–7.

7 J. P. Cooper, 'Henry VII's last years reconsidered', *Historical Journal*, ii. (1959), 117.

8 *Ibid.*, p.118.

9 E1 2655, fo.7.

10 *Ibid.*, fo.8.

11 G. R. Elton, 'Henry VII: a restatement', *H.J.*, iv. (1961), 23.

12 E1 2655, fo.8.

13 *Ibid.*, fo.7.

14 Elton, 'Henry VII', p.23.

15 E1 2655, fos.7–9v.; Lansdowne 639, fos.25–44v.

16 Lansdowne 639, fos.25–44v.; 2/1/92, 3/54, 7/75–87, 89–92, 148, 199–202, 14/141–3, 144–5, 20/15, 29/fragments, 32/fragments.

17 2/2/206–9; 10/4, Pt. 2.

18 E.g. by the present author in *E.H.R.*, xci (1976), 481.

19 *LP* i. 218(44).

20 J. A. Guy, 'The Court of Star Chamber during Wolsey's Ascendancy' (Cambridge Ph.D. thesis, 1973), appendix ii.

21 E1 2652, fo.3v.

22 E1 2655, fo.10.

23 *Illustrations of British History . . . in the Reigns of Henry VIII, Edward VI, Mary, Elizabeth, and James I,* ed. E. Lodge (London, 1838), i. 13.

24 B.M. Cotton MS., Vespasian C. xiv (Pt. 2), fo.266v.

25 *Infra,* p. 67.

26 Lodge, *Illustrations,* i.13.

27 E1 2655, fo.15.

28 E1 2655, fos.9v.–18v.; 2/17/406, 21/232, 24/130, 29/fragments; 10/4, Pt. 2; SP 1/18, fo.223v. (*LP* iii. 365); SP 1/33, fos.165–6 (*LP* iv. 1082); SP 1/232 (Pt. 1), fo.59 (*LP Add.* i. 206); SP 1/234 (Pt. 2), fos.118–19 (*LP Add.* i. 430); Lansdowne 639, fos. 46v.–49; Lansdowne 1, fo.108.

29 E.g. W. H. Dunham, 'Henry VIII's Whole Council and its Parts', *Huntington Library Quarterly,* vii (1943), 7–46; 'The Ellesmere Extracts from the Acta Consilii of King Henry VIII', *E.H.R.,* lviii (1943), 301–18; 'The Members of Henry VIII's Whole Council, 1509–27', *E.H.R.,* lix. (1944), 187–210; 'Wolsey's Rule of the King's Whole Council', *American Historical Review,* xlix. (1944), 644–62.

30 Guy, 'The Court of Star Chamber', appendix i.

31 *Ibid.*, appendix ii.

32 Lodge, *Illustrations,* i.22–3; Brewer's *Preface* in *LP* i. (2nd ed.), Pt. 3, liv–vi.

33 Guy, 'The Court of Star Chamber', appendix i.

34 As n. 28 *supra*; 2/15/188–90; *Tudor Royal Proclamations,* i, *The Early Tudors 1485–1553,* ed. P. L. Hughes and J. F. Larkin (New Haven, 1964), 172–4.

35 E1 2655, fo.9v.
36 Lodge, *Illustrations*, i.9; E1 2655, fos.9v.–10.
37 E1 2655, fo.10; E1 2654, fos.22v.–23.
38 *Ibid.*
39 *Infra*, p.68.
40 Lodge, *Illustrations*, i.13–14.
41 *Ibid.*, p.28.
42 2/16/365–72, 2/18/161.
43 Lodge, *Illustrations*, i.27–28.
44 2/16/365–72.
45 KB 29/148, *roti.* 6–8, 17, 43, 44.
46 E1 2654, fos.23v.–24. The correct date is established by C 82/448.
47 *Ibid.*; E. Hall, *The Triumphant Reigne of Kyng Henry the VIII*, ed. C. Whibley (London, 1904), i.163–4. The chronicler mistook the day of the event.
48 E1 2654, fos.23v.–24.
49 E1 2655, fo.15.
50 *Infra*, pp. 72–4.
51 SP 1/14, fos.108–13 (*LP* ii. 2579). The date is established by E1 2652, fo.7.
52 SP 1/14, fo.111.
53 E1 2655, fo.10.
54 SP 1/14, fo.113.
55 E1 2652, fo.7.
56 C 254/161/31, 33; cf. *English Historical Documents, 1327–1485*, ed. A. R. Myers (London, 1969), 555–6.
57 E1 2655, fo.15v.
58 E1 2652, fo.3; KB 29/148, *roti.* 44, 51–5; Keilway, *Reports d'ascuns Cases*, fos.188, 192, 194–6.
59 *LP* ii. 2684.
60 Keilway, fos.190–2; E1 2655, fo.11v.; Lansdowne 639, fos.44v.–45.
61 E1 2655, fo.13.
62 E1 2655, fo.15v.; 2/26/355, 395, 17/347.
63 E1 2655, fo.15v.
64 *Infra*, pp. 61–7.
65 Hall, *Henry the VIII*, i.152; Brewer's *Preface*, p.liii.
66 *Supra*, p.27; Lansdowne 639, fos.45v.–46.
67 *Infra*, p.76–8.
68 *Infra*, pp.72–4.

69 *Infra,* pp. 68–9.
70 A. F. Pollard, *Wolsey* (London, 1929), 74.
71 Cf. *LP* iv. 5750 (p.2562).
72 Pollard, pp.74–5.
73 SP 1/16, fo.16v. (*LP* ii. App.38).
74 *Ibid.*
75 Pollard, p.73; *LP* ii. 3973.
76 Pollard, p.75; *LP* iii. App.21.
77 Giustinian declared that Wolsey had 'the reputation of being extremely just: he favours the people exceedingly, and especially the poor; hearing their suits, and seeking to despatch them instantly; he also makes the lawyers plead gratis for all paupers'; *Four Years at the Court of Henry VIII,* translated by R. Brown (London, 1854), ii.314.
78 *Infra,* p.81.
79 Hall, *Henry the VIII,* i.152.
80 *Infra,* pp.53–8.
81 *Infra,* pp.103–5.
82 The council was so styled in its judicial capacity early in Wolsey's ascendancy; 2/3/79–82.
83 E1 2653; E1 2654, fos.22v.–25; E1 2655, fos.9v.–18v.; 10/4, Pt. 2; 10/18; 2/17/406, 21/232, 24/130, 29/fragments, 35/21; Lansdowne 639, fos.46v.–49; Lansdowne 160, fos.309v.–12; Lansdowne 1, fo.108.
84 *Infra,* pp.79–109.
85 Lansdowne 1, fo.108. The correct date is established by Lansdowne 639, fo.48v.
86 Lansdowne 1, fo.108; Lansdowne 639, fo.54v.; E1 2652, fo.4v.
87 As n. 106 *infra.*
88 Lansdowne 160, fos.310v.–11; 2/17/389, 8/49–50, 25/283, 1/76, 4/98–108, 21/45, 23/252.
89 Lansdowne 160, fos.310v.–11.
90 As n. 87 *supra*; SP 1/231, fos.95–6 (*LP Add.* 64).
91 *Ibid.*
92 Lansdowne 160, fo.311.
93 *Ibid.*
94 *Ibid.*
95 2/8/49–50.
96 2/4/100.
97 *Ibid.*
98 2/21/45.

99 Lansdowne 160, fos. 310v.–11; 2/25/283.

100 *Ibid.*

101 *Infra,* pp. 97–105.

102 Guy, 'The Court of Star Chamber', p.106.

103 The major sources for conciliar personnel and activity outside star chamber in this period are, first, the council registers, which survive in the P.R.O. as REQ 1/4–5, 104–5; secondly, the proceedings before the councillors. Official endorsements on these proceedings are far more extensive and informative than those on star chamber documents. On this point, cf. the note which follows the record of an admission of 24 April 1521 in REQ 1/104, fo.110: *'postea compromissa fuit causa ut supra billas'.* However, since these proceedings could not, for obvious reasons, be identified as proceedings of the court of requests, the staff of the P.R.O. bundled them up for the most part amongst the vast miscellanea of that court, REQ 3, where they now lie unlisted and accessible only in bundles. To facilitate present identification, therefore, references to this miscellanea will include particulars of the principal parties in the suits and indicate where necessary the nature of individual documents in question.

104 REQ 1/4, fo.3.

105 E.g. REQ 3/4: *Russell* v. *Jolys;* REQ 3/7: *Prior of Wenloke* v. *Lakyn, Brasebrigge* v. *Cartwright, Wylson* v. *Raynold;* REQ 3/10: *Symmes* v. *Bekford, Clifford* v. *Clifford.*

106 E.g. REQ 3/2: *Ballyswell* v. *Lovell, Alyson* v. *Rose;* REQ 3/4: *Byrchenshaw* v. *earl of Derby;* REQ 3/5: *Clerke* v. *Barnard, Cosse* v. *Longe;* REQ 3/6: *Tolby* v. *Knyghtley, Curson* v. *Brykkes.*

107 REQ 1/4, fos.3–136v.

108 E1 2652, fo.11; E1 2655, fos.12, 16; E1 2658; SP 1/19, fo.143 (*LP* iii. 571). Cf. Pollard, pp.84–5.

109 Pollard, pp.88–9.

110 Few plaintiffs in the council courts were ever in the poverty bracket, despite claims to the contrary, though some were genuine paupers, e.g. REQ 1/5, fo.63v.; *Bayne* v. *Tyrwhyt,* REQ 3/5. Moreover, it could be tactically very unwise to assume false poverty, since a discovery to the contrary by the court could be made the ground for a dismissal to the common law. Thus one John Porter, who pleaded that he was 'poor' and 'not of power to sue for his remedye' at law, was dismissed in 1519: 'fforasmoche as it apperethe unto the kinges Counsaill that the playntyff . . . ys a gent., havyng landes and tenementes to hym dissended, suf-

ficient and able to maynteigne and folowe hys suete and clayme
. . . after the order and course of the kinges commyn lawes' (*Porter* v. *Mathewe,* REQ 3/5).

111 SP 1/19, fo.143 (*LP* iii. 571); for the date, E1 2652, fo.11.
112 E1 2655, fo.12.
113 E1 2655, fo.16.
114 Hall, *Henry the VIII,* i.153.
115 *Broke* v. *Bradbury,* REQ 3/5. Endorsement on bill of complaint: '*Coram domino Abbate Westm' et aliis de consilio. Et quia non Agitur de causis commissis eisdem, committantur domino decano capelle &c'*.
116 E.g. REQ 3/8: *Vardon* v. *Bulkeley;* REQ 3/9: *Downe* v. *Lucy;* REQ 3/10: *Love* v. *Tolly, Longbothom* v. *Saville.*
117 REQ 1/105, fo.lv.; REQ 3/4: *Dowker* v. *Shelton, Arnold* v. *Studholse, Holdeson* v. *Mowtyng;* REQ 3/5: *Porter* v. *Mathewe;* REQ 3/8: *Mirthe* v. *Aldeworth;* REQ 3/10: *Pante* v. *Knyght, Longbothom* v. *Saville.*
118 REQ 1/104, fos.68v., 88v.
119 Not to be confused with York Place, the modern Whitehall.
120 REQ 1/4, fos.139–54; REQ 1/5, fos.3v.–71. Pressing matters might still, however, be heard in vacation; cf. the endorsement on the defendant's answer in *Palmer* v. *Clif,* REQ 3/6.
121 REQ 1/5, fo.20.
122 REQ 1/5, fo.22.
123 Cf. G. R. Elton, *The Tudor Revolution in Government,* (Cambridge, 1953), 64.
124 E.g. REQ 3/5: *Smyth* v. *Ovy;* REQ 3/6: *Turnour* v. *Samon, Martyn* v. *Tunstead;* REQ 3/9: *Stower* v. *Squier;* REQ 3/10: *Rokes* v. *Eggecombe;* loose leaf inserted into REQ 1/5 as fo. 24.
125 *Infra,* p.147 n.104.
126 E.g. documents in cases cited at n. 122 *supra.*
127 A study of the numerous examples to be found scattered through the early bundles of REQ 3, and the endorsements on pleadings which ordered their composition and issue, could have avoided unnecessary confusion on this point. Cf. Bayne, pp.lxxxvii–viii.
128 REQ 1/104, fo.58. This entry is undated, but the date assigned here is most likely: the suit was still depending in Michaelmas term 1520, when the defendant was ordered to keep his daily appearance.
129 E.g. REQ 1/104, fos.132v., 135v., 137v., 138v., 143v.; REQ 3/3: *Browne* v. *Myll;* REQ 3/4: *Arnold* v. *Studholse;* REQ 3/5: *Sutton* v. *Turner, Slak* v. *Colisen.*

130 E.g. entries for June 1521: REQ 1/104, fos.135v., 137v., 138v., 143v., 145v., 146, 146v., 147v. Cf. Hall, *Henry the VIII*, i. 152.

131 Stated by Roger Orgor, priest, in his bill of complaint to Wolsey, REQ 3/1.

132 E1 2652, fo.4v., and the argument set out in the decree of 26 April 1521 in *Burwasshe* v. *Honychurche*, REQ 3/10. Actions in king's bench on Magna Carta and 42 Edw. III, c.3, concerning proceedings which had been before Stokesley, are found (undetermined) on KB 27/1048, *ro*. 75, and KB 27/1050, *ro*.47. I am grateful to Dr J. H. Baker for these references.

133 Lansdowne 639, fo.56v.

134 Stated by Orgor.

135 SP 1/37, fos.65–103 (*LP* iv. 1939); *A Collection of Ordinances and Regulations for the Government of the Royal Household* (London, Society of Antiquaries, 1790), 159–60; G. R. Elton, *The Tudor Constitution* (Cambridge, 1962), 90, 93–4.

136 Elton, *Tudor Revolution*, p.321.

137 *Household Ordinances*, p.160.

138 Elton, *Tudor Revolution*, pp.347–50.

139 SP 1/59, fo.77 (*LP* iv. App.67); SP 1/235 (Pt. 1),.fo.37 (*LP Add.* 481).

140 *Ibid.*

141 E1 2655, fo.18; E1 2652, fo.10; Pollard, pp.89–90.

142 E1 2655, fo.18.

143 *Ibid.*

144 E1 2652, fo.10; cf. *Plomer* v. *Warde*, REQ 3/9.

145 *Ibid.*; the specified counties are stated in the ms. Richmond's council was given both administrative and judicial authority in all the shires north of the Trent, save Durham; R. R. Reid, *The King's Council in the North* (London, 1921), 108.

146 *Infra*, pp. 102–4.

147 E.g. *Foliambe* v. *Porte*, 2/15/141–9; *Bulle* v. *Carant*, 2/5/72–6, 3/51; *Dawe* v. *Chaynay*, REQ 3/1; *Holdeson* v. *Mowtyng*, REQ 3/4.

148 *Infra*, pp.103–4.

149 *Ibid.*

150 E1 2652, fo.10.

151 *Ibid.*

152 E.g. *Dallowe* v. *Pygott*, 2/12/46–65, 19/78, 17/386; *Owen* v. *Coole*, 2/19/178; *Philip* v. *Holford*, 2/20/328; *Plomer* v. *Warde*, REQ 3/9; *Clayton* v. *Trevor*, 2/10/41, 17/73; *Dobbyns* v. *Morton*, 2/12/221–4.

153 *LP* iv. 2201; *Tudor Royal Proclamations*, i.153–4; cf. Pollard, pp.90,

92. The evidence of the record does not bear out the statement made in Sir Thomas Elyot's famous letter of 1532 to Cromwell; Elyot was seeking preferment, having been impoverished by an expensive lawsuit, and greatly exaggerated; B.M. Cotton MS. Titus B. i, fos.376–7 (*LP* v. 1617).

154 SP 1/46, fo.252 (*LP* iv. 3926); cf. Lansdowne 639, fo.59; *Bulletin of the Institute of Historical Research,* v. (1927), 23–7. The date is established by E1 2652, fo.13, which duplicates the remainder of the entry for the day.

155 E1 2652, fo.4v.

156 REQ 1/5, fo.43v.

157 The remainder were Dr Rowland Philips, vicar of Croydon, Dr Roger Lupton, provost of Eton, Dr Edward Cromer, Sir Thomas Neville, Sir William Sulyard, Christopher Saint-Germain, John Islip, abbot of Westminster, Dr Henry Standish, bishop of St Asaph, Sir William Weston, prior of St John, Sir John Husye, Sir William Fitzwilliam, Sir Roger Townesend.

158 REQ 1/5, fos.44ff.

CHAPTER 3

1 These extracts, notes and other sources are fully described in my article in *Journal of the Society of Archivists,* v (1975), 175–80.

2 On the technical problems presented by the *Star Chamber Proceedings, ibid.,* pp.170–3.

3 *Supra,* pp.15–16.

4 This account of common law development relies on S.F.C. Milsom, *Historical Foundations of the Common Law* (London, 1969), 127–39; A. W. B. Simpson, *An Introduction to the History of the Land Law* (Oxford, 1961), 34–43.

5 Littleton, cited in Simpson, p.39.

6 Milsom, p.134. Thus, in 1334 a claimaint was hauled out by his heels when half-way through a window, and an assize on this determined the validity of a deed of grant.

7 5 Ric. II, St. 1, c.8; 15 Ric. II, c.2; 4 Hen. IV, c.8; 8 Hen. VI, c.9.

8 Milsom, p.132; Simpson, p.136.

9 E.g. *Cawodlegh* v. *Coryton,* 2/26/26, 253, 301, 304, 20/85; *Freman* v. *Brokyns,* 2/24/161; *Gibson* v. *Gilberte,* 2/18/166; *Heselerton* v. *Heselerton,* 2/30/139; *Smyth* v. *Sampson,* 2/22/314; *Thursbye* v. *Coverte,* 2/18/98.

10 E.g. *Frechewell* v. *Lowe*, 2/19/27; *Heed* v. *Franke*, 2/19/198.

11 E.g. *Agarde* v. *Corbet*, 2/1/36–7; *Cantrell* v. *Tatton*, 2/24/26, 18/326; *Curwen* v. *Belyngeham*, 2/11/104–29; *Percey* v. *Somervyle*, 2/35/58. *Bayly* v. *Wallope*, 2/20/309, 334, 17/45, 19/388.

12 *Dodd* v. *Bromley*, 2/12/238–9, 243, 245–6.

13 2/12/246.

14 *Infra*, pp. 97–105.

15 *Infra*, pp.96–7.

16 *Alatt* v. *Nowell*, 2/1/67; *Toft* v. *Thomas*, 10/4, Pt. 2; Lansdowne 639, fo.38.

17 *Grey* v. *Compton*, 2/16/295–312, 26/48, 260, 10/141–3.

18 E.g. *Tunstall* v. *Sterky*, 2/30/126; *Alatt* v. *Stenynges*, 2/1/39; 10/4, Pt. 2; *infra*, p.126.

19 Cf. Harleian 2143, fo.69.

20 E1 2652, fos.1, 9.

21 E1 2652, fo.9; 2/31/fragments.

22 2/27/81; *infra*, p.97.

23 2/12/150.

24 *Ibid.*

25 E1 2652, fo.17; cf. Harleian 2143, fo.1v.

26 An exception would be made, for example, in an instance of 'inequality' of the parties: the one side poor, the other gentle and much 'friended'; E1 2652, fo.17v.; *Webbe* v. *Runyon* (and cross-suit), 4/5/52, 2/15.

27 E1 2768, fo.29v.; Additional 37,045, fos.49v.–50.

28 E1 2768, fo.29v.; Harleian 2143, fo.1.

29 E.g. *Peers* v. *Taway*, 2/27/171; *Warre* v. *Abbot of Bermondesey*, 2/17/160; *Torre* v. *Lytton*, 2/31/125; *Benger* v. *Stanley*, 2/4/206, 214–16, 20/249; *Horpole* v. *Wodegate*, 2/21/61.

30 *Wyllys* v. *Newname*, 2/23/209.

31 E.g. *Abbots of Ford and Tintern* v. *Poyntz*, 2/17/259, 19/305, 20/7, 24/67, 25/203, 31/fragments; *Amadas* v. *Kendall*, 2/1/149, 26/257; *Brenner* v. *Clement*, 2/20/385; *Merynge* v. *Spratt*, 2/27/47; *Sturtyvant* v. *Hatfeld*, 2/20/228, 25/36; *Talbott* v. *Lord Monteagle*, 2/26/345; *Abbot of Tavistock* v. *Harries*, 2/30/115.

32 *Supra*, p.34.

33 'Allegatum est per principalem Justiciarum quod riotta iudicanda est ex modo collecto turbe, et non ex genere armorum. Ideo quando quis aliquid attemptat cum turba collecta ultra consuetum numerum sese commitantium sive cum armis, vel siné, riottum facit'; Bayne, pp.19–20. That the 'wonted number' of

persons had to be above two was implicit in every decision in riot; it was explicit as the accepted rule in *Lodge* v. *Lodge,* Additional 37,045, fo.2v.

34 E.g. SP 1/59, fo.127 (*LP* iv. App.176). E1 2652, fo.13v.

35 E1 2652, fos.7v., 12v.

36 E1 2768, fo.28.

37 E1 2652, fo.7v.

38 *Ibid.*

39 W. G. Searle, *The History of the Queens' College* (Cambridge, 1867), 168–9. The original bill of complaint was to Wolsey and the queen's council; but it was referred to star chamber.

40 *Ibid.*

41 E1 2652, fo.7v.

42 *Ibid.*

43 *Thornham* v. *Calthrope,* 2/18/99.

44 *Coker* v. *Baskett,* 2/10/72–82, 9/138–48 (2 suits).

45 *Abbot of Mychelney* v. *Langdon,* 2/18/303.

46 ———— v. *Abbot of Byndon,* 2/1/28–30.

47 2/12/260–309.

48 *Supra,* p.31.

49 2/12/261. The informations were left pending in king's bench.

50 2/12/262.

51 2/12/263.

52 2/12/261.

53 2/12/262.

54 2/12/265–71.

55 *Saunders* v. *Debenham,* 2/17/237; ———— v. *Darstyn,* 2/18/96; E1 2652, fo.10v; SP 1/46, fos.251–2 (*LP* iv. 3926); 2/29/fragments.

56 *Atkynson* v. *Flete,* 2/2/150.

57 Only part of this story was retrieved by G. R. Elton, *Policy and Police* (Cambridge, 1972), 313–14; the documents in the case are 2/19/302, 30/fragments; E1 2655, fo.16v.; Lansdowne 639, fo.56.

58 2/30/fragments.

59 E1 2655, fo.16v.

60 *Ibid.*

61 2/19/302.

62 CP 40/1033, *roti.* 322, 430; CP 40/1035, *ro.* 434. I am indebted to Dr J. H. Baker for drawing these references to my attention.

63 E1 2655, fo.16v.

64 2/19/302.

65 *Ibid.*

66 2/30/fragments.

67 E.g. *Attorney-general* v. *Cheseman et al.*, 2/2/156–7; *Attorney-general*
v. *Payn et al.*, 2/2/205; *Attorney-general* v. *Bevell et al.*, 3/6/56; *Attorney-general* v. *Symson et al.*, 3/6/57.

68 E1 495, 2657; E1 2652, fos.10v., 17v., 18v.; Harleian 2143, fos. 5,
9v., 10, 14, 51, 140, 152, 167, 189.

69 E1 2652, fos. 6v., 13v.

70 E1 2655, fo.17v.

71 E1 2652, fo.6v.

72 E1 2652, fo.13v.

73 *Dene* v. *Banaster*, 2/12/186; *Tailour* v. *Cholmeley*, 2/30/109; *Sadeler*
v. *Cacher*, 2/19/138; *Kelke* v. *Gyrlyngton*, 2/23/66, 20/363, 24/153,
22/276; *Booth* v. *Davenport*, 2/5/135, 164–5.

74 *Huncote* v. *Hamond*, 2/19/158; *Sweteman* v. *Brereton*, 2/3/311,
17/227, 185, 18/162, 19/81, 22/113, 24/434, 26/370; *Jankyn* v.
Longhour, 2/25/209.

75 *Jenkyns* v. *Ap William*, 2/24/3. The plaintiff explained that an
appeal of murder did not lie after eight years.

76 *Anysley* v *Grey*, 2/1/181.

77 *Nelar* v. *Abbot of Tavistock*, 2/31/53; *Vaughan* v. *Ap Meredeth*,
2/19/383.

78 *Rokeby* v. *Constable*, 2/29/44; SP 1/34, fos.5–8 (*LP* iv. 1115);
Hogeson v. *Constable*, 2/20/144; *Tutt* v. *Irishe*, 2/35/4; *Warterton* v.
Leke, 2/26/201; *Mordaunt* v. *Tyler*, 2/26/401; *Genysford* v. *Morgan*,
2/16/65–6.

79 SP 1/34, fos.5–8. He was pardoned in February 1525 (*LP* iv.
1136 [22]). Anne Grisacre became successively ward and
daughter-in-law of Sir Thomas More.

80 *Parishioners of Much Waltham* v. *Cornyshe*, 2/10/261–2, 23/35,
28/fragments; 10/4, Pt. 2; Lansdowne 639, fo.55.

81 *Fenymere* v. *Waller*, 2/15/40, 24/25.

82 *Pole* v. *Brett*, 2/19/312.

83 E1 2652, fo.13.

84 An instance of the council's being called upon to investigate
crime in an executive capacity is SP 1/11, fo.82 (*LP* ii. 911).

85 E.g. SP 1/21, fos.125–6 (*LP* iii. 1065); Lansdowne 639, fo.55v.

86 E1 2652, fo.8v.

87 *Alatt* v. *Stenynges*, 2/1/39; *A Maryk* v. *Cave*, 2/1/150; *Balle* v.
Newdegate, 2/3/52–3; *Holdforth* v. *Holdforth*, 2/21/40, 24/337,

26/82; *Tenants of Temple Sowerby* v. *Crakenthorp*, 2/31/44; *Flemmyng* v. *Bellew*, 2/20/315.

88 E1 2652, fo.8v.; E1 2655, fo.13; Lansdowne 639, fo.35; *infra*, pp.128–9.

89 Bayne, pp.cxxvii–ix.

90 E1 2652, fo.7.

91 E1 2652, fo.3.

92 SP 1/59, fos.149–50 (*LP* iv. App.242).

93 *Inhabitants of Bungay* v. *Wharton*, 2/7/194, 26/456.

94 *Rychars* v. *Wharton*, 2/18/194, 132, 17/362, 20/238, 22/261, 26/456, 20/95, 31/fragments; *Dowsyng* v. *Wharton*, 2/24/344, 25/148; *Fuller* v. *Wharton*, 2/15/270–1, 23/306, 24/409, 26/307, 22/179; *Southall* v. *Wharton*, 2/18/295, 19/238, 20/32, 70, 25/179; *Wace* v. *Wharton*, 2/23/21; *Lynde* v. *Wharton*, 2/23/63, 150, 153; *Coseler* v. *Wharton*, 2/5/161; *Denham* v. *Wharton*, 2/4/109; 10/4 Pt. 2.

95 *Wharton* v. *Rychars, Dowsyng and Fuller*, 2/19/92, 99, 185; *Gyrlyng* v. *Southall*, 2/25/101, 16/70.

96 2/20/70.

97 E1 2652, fos.2, 12.

98 *Jenkynson* v. *Salisbury*, 2/1/4–5.

99 Bayne, pp.clx–xv.

100 Leadam, *Star Chamber 1509–1544*, p.111.

101 It should, however, be noted that the council was much concerned with liberties and franchises, municipalities, and economic matters in its executive capacity. E.g. 2/13/204, 24/50, 15/188–90; SP 1/232, Pt. 1, fos.58–69 (*LP Add.* 206); E1 2652, fo.7; E1 2655, *passim*.

102 *Pulleyn* v. *Mayor of York* (and cross-suit), 2/17/287, 19/178.

103 *Bailiffs of Tewkesbury* v. *Nasshe*, 2/31/118.

104 2/25/63.

105 *Mayor of Waterford* v. *Citizens of New Ross*, 2/23/20.

106 *Mayor of Newcastle* v. *Gild Merchants of Newcastle*, 2/24/307; Lansdowne 639, fo.45; Leadam, pp.68–118.

107 Leadam, p.108.

108 *Ibid.*, p.c.

109 *Ibid.*, pp.111–16.

110 *Dale* v. *Mayor of Bristol*, 2/6/78–85; Leadam, pp.142–65.

111 Leadam, p.143.

112 *Ibid.*, p.149.

113 *Ibid.*, p.cxviii.

114 *Ibid.*, pp.163–5.

115 *Prior and Convent of Norwich* v. *Mayor and Commonalty of City of Norwich*, 2/23/268, 34/21, 27/fragments.

116 *The History of the City and County of Norwich* (Norwich, 1768), 127–8.

117 C 44/37B.

118 Bayne, p.clxi.

119 *History of Norwich*, p.143.

120 SP 1/21, fos.145–58 (*LP* iii. 1113); 2/23/268).

121 *The Records of the City of Norwich*, ed. W. Hudson and J. C. Tingey (Norwich, 1910), ii. 370–1.

122 SP 1/29, fos.236–90 (*LP* iii. App.12); SP 1/32, fo.70 (*LP* iv. 655); C 66/644, m.26 (*LP* iv. 741, 770); C 66/645, m.14 (*LP* iv. 895 [10]).

123 2/24/21; 27/fragments.

124 C 82/560; Additional 5,949 (*LP* iv. 1366). *History of Norwich*, pp.169–70. For some reason the letters patent were not enrolled: no doubt because of a dispute as to who should pay the fees for the enrolment.

125 *Cordwainers Company of London* v. *Alien Cordwainers*, 2/2/44, 9/184, 15/318, 31/140, 10/230; SP 1/55, fos.240–1 (*LP* iv. 6028); *Jenans* v. *Pursell*, 2/25/275; *Foliambe* v. *Revell*, 2/15/150, 23/307 (2 suits); *Simondes* v. *Whitehead*, 2/34/10, 24/300.

126 E.g. SP 1/232 Pt. 1, fos.58–69 (*LP Add.* 206); E1 2655, *passim*.

127 2/26/103; E1 2655, fo.16.

128 *Tudor Royal Proclamations*, ed. P. L. Hughes and J. F. Larkin (New Haven, 1964), i.172.

129 *Ibid.*, p. 173.

130 *Barett (or Bareth)* v. *Newby*, 2/22/340; Leadam, p. 169.

131 *Ibid.*, p. 174.

132 *Constables of Yaxley* v. *Alward*, 2/23/104, 17/344; Leadam, p. 179.

133 *Ibid.*

134 *Inhabitants of Great Massingham* v. *Prior of Westacre*, 2/29/187; *Gaynesforde* v. *Lewkenner*, 2/16/35; *Lloyd* v. *Gryffyth*, 2/23/168; *A Wood* v. *Clymhoo*, 2/31/100.

135 *Ferdynandy* v *Clerk*, 2/15/45–6; *Ferdynandy* v. *Bucland*, 2/15/47–8; *Kepar* v. *White*, 2/23/125; *Fenton* v. *Hert*, 2/20/293.

136 *Attwoode* v. *Cattellyn*, 2/2/225–7.

137 *Calybutt* v. *Lovell*, 2/9/27–8, 17/263; *Prioress of Stratforde and Halywell* v. *Abbot of Stratforde*, 2/18/111 *Abbot of Furness* v. *Tunstall*, 2/15/281–2; *Brewer* v. *Legh*, 2/18/79; *Lord Lisle* v. *Cobley*,

2/10/66–7.

138 *Smyth* v. *Fletcher*, 2/31/36; *Wright* v. *Mounson*, 2/32/73; *Burdon* v. *Taylboys*, 2/7/195; *Dunwyche* v. *Lucas*, 2/13/149; *Fuliambe* v. *Revell*, 2/23/307.

139 *Owen* v. *Auncell*, 2/31/177; *Countess of Oxford* v. *Coopyng*, 2/28/2; *Countess of Oxford* v. *Rockewoode*, 2/27/113.

140 *Wastell* v. *Bradborne*, 2/13/144; *Prior of Bradenestoke* v. *Anne*, 2/6/268; *Brome* v. *Curson*, 2/6/176, 22/352; *Inhabitants of Draycott and Stoke-Gifford* v. *Rodney*, 2/13/83–4; *Tenants of Fakenham* v. *Fermor*, 2/15/11–13; *Hatfield* v. *Sturtyvant*, 2/30/46.

141 *Colet* v. *Parson of Pakelsham*, 2/9/159; *Pygott* v. *Prior of Basingwarke*, 2/18/45.

142 *Brereton* v. *Swetnam*, 2/20/175.

143 *Legh* v. *Massy*, 2/21/197.

144 *Hall* v. *Slowght*, 2/25/325; *Warner* v. *Baxter*, 2/23/54; *Hampton* v. *Abbot of Abingdon*, 2/23/238.

145 *Tenants of Gower* v. *Cradock*, 2/16/190–6; *Duke of Buckingham* v. *Tenants of Brecknock and Hay*, 2/35/21; *Bayly* v. *Lord Mountjoy*, 2/3/249–53; 10/4 Pt. 2.

146 The cases variously appear in E1 2652–5; Lansdowne 639; Hall, *Henry the VIII*, i.180, ii.46. The proceedings against the earl of Northumberland (*supra*, p. 27) and Thomas lord Dacre (*infra*, pp. 122–23) have not, perhaps wrongly, been classified as official prosecutions. Although the earl's appearance in star chamber on 2 May 1516 may have been on a par with that of Sir William Bulmer, which has been counted, his submission was for contempt of the council's jurisdiction in private suits (Lansdowne 639, fo.45v.). This not infrequent offence was traditionally dealt with in summary form by the council. Lord Dacre's 'acknowledgment' of his administrative malfeasance in 1525 is more difficult. No information could be filed against him, as in the cases of the Surrey justices, since there had been no official investigation. The complaints against him were, indeed, those of private persons. When Dacre's conduct was debated in his presence by the council, he short-circuited the proceedings by confession and submission, eventually making fine with the king in 1,500 marks. Wolsey and the council were acting in a primarily executive capacity: Dacre was brought to answer the complaints, and compounded to avoid an official prosecution. Should this view appear over-sophisticated, however, the episode could be added to the count of official suits.

147 *Supra*, pp. 61–3, 64–5.
148 2/26/355, 24/29.
149 2/2/163.
150 2/2/178, 194.
151 *Attorney-General* v. *Browne*, 2/2/163, 183–4, 18/246, 26/252, 22/50; *Attorney-General* v. *A. Legh*, 2/2/194–7; *Attorney-General* v. *Howard*, 2/2/178–82; 10/4, Pt. 5.
152 2/18/246.
153 2/2/195–6.
154 2/2/179–82.
155 2/2/179.
156 Cotton MS. Vespasian C. xiv (Pt. 2), fo.266v.
157 E1 2654, fo.24v.; E1 2653.
158 E1 2655, fo.15.
159 E1 2655, fo.14v.
160 E1 2654, fo.24v. This episode was the prelude to Wolsey's destruction of Stafford, achieved in 1521; cf. *LP* iii, pp. 492, 494.
161 E1 2654, fo.24v.
162 *Ibid.*
163 11 Hen. VII, c.7.
164 The statute was scheduled to endure only to the next parliament, but the procedure was operating in 1511; E1 2652, fo.7v. Cf. Bayne, pp. cxxx–i.
165 E1 2655, fo.18; Hall, *Henry the VIII*, ii.46.
166 Lansdowne 639, fo.58.
167 E1 2652, fo.10v.; Lansdowne 639, fo.45.
168 Cf. *LP* ii. 4124.
169 W. E. Wilkie, *The Cardinal Protectors of England* (Cambridge, 1974), 105–6.
170 Pollard, p.194.
171 Lansdowne 639, fo.46v.; SP 1/16, fo.225 (*LP* ii. 4072).
172 Lansdowne 639, fos.47, 54; SP 1/16, fos.35–6 (*LP* ii. 3741), wrongly dated by Richard Lee (clerk of the council); 2/1/94–6; E1 2655, fos.12–13.
173 E1 2655, fos.12.
174 2/1/96.
175 *Ibid.*; SP 1/16, fo.35.
176 Pollard, pp. 193–4; Sir H. Ellis, *Original Letters*, 3rd series (London, 1846), ii.41–2.
177 2/2/75; E1 2655, fo.13v.
178 E1 2655, fo.13v.

179 2/2/75.
180 Pollard, ch.2.
181 Pollard, p.48.
182 El 2655, fo.13v.
183 10/4, Pt. 2; SP 1/16, fos.141–3 (*LP* ii, 3951); 2/17/227.
184 Pollard, pp.45, 52.
185 C 54/386; cf. E 36/216, fo.176.
186 10/4, Pt. 2; *LP* ii. 3487.
187 10/4, Pt. 2.
188 *Ibid.*
189 *Ibid.*
190 *LP* ii, 2537.
191 10/4, Pt. 2. That a pardon was not valid in murder, treason and rape unless the offence was specified was settled by 13 Ric. II, St. 2, c.1.
192 10/4, Pt. 2.
193 *Ibid.*
194 *Ibid.*
195 Pollard, p.52.

CHAPTER 4

1 William West, *The Second Part of Symboleography* (London, 1627), 194.
2 E.g. discovery, enforcement of uses, relief from inequitable contracts, or specific performance; Bayne, p.lxxxi. In cases where plaintiffs gave reasons for seeking remedy in star chamber, the commonest claims were that they were too poor to sue at common law, being impoverished as a result of the activities of defendants, or could have no successful outcome at law for similar reasons.
3 Cf. Bayne, p.lxxx. During the period of Henry VIII's absence in 1520 (31 May–c. 16 July), bills of complaint were addressed to Thomas Howard, duke of Norfolk, in his capacity as regent.
4 West, p.194.
5 2/27/fragments.
6 E.g. *Ap Gruff* v. *Gryffith*, 2/33/44; *Sely* v. *Middelmore*, 32/97;

Skynner v. *Fuliambe*, 23/24; Velavyle's information, 17/347.

7 E.g. *Holt* v. *Tyndale*, 2/21/84; *Olyver* v. *Gybbys*, 21/158; *Savell* v. *Tempest*, 18/153, 328, 22/201, 24/238; *Ferrers* v. *Gruffith*, 18/234.

8 West, p.183; 15 Hen. VI, c.4.

9 E1 2652, fo.1v.

10 Lansdowne 639, fos.30, 31 (twice).

11 E.g. *Astymer* v. *Bulwar*, 2/2/148; *Barker* v. *Flynte*, 33/15; *Bayly* v. *Thomas*, 3/314; *Beauchamp* v. *Banathlek*, 4/2.

12 E1 2652, fo.11v.

13 The single exception seems to have been in *Barett* v. *Newby*, 2/22/340. In the exchequer, all persons laying informations except the attorney-general were required to swear to the truth of their statements; Bayne, p.lxxxiv.

14 E1 2652, fo.11v. In fairness to Wolsey, the practice may be detected in operation in 1514; Bayne, p.lxxxiv, and *Entwysell* v. *Kyngston*, 2/14/141–3. The abuse later became common to star chamber, chancery and requests. Even Sir Thomas Egerton's vigorous attempt to restrain the method failed; Lansdowne 639, fo.lv.

15 W. J. Jones, *The Elizabethan Court of Chancery* (Oxford, 1967), 192 n. 1.

16 E1 2652, fos.11v., 17; Jones, pp.27–36.

17 Lansdowne 639, fos.41v., 44v.

18 E1 2652, fo.11v.

19 Baldwin, *King's Council*, p.288.

20 *Ibid.*, p.290 n.1.

21 E.g. examples in 2/27/fragments; 10/4, Pt. 2; REQ 3/4.

22 Bayne, pp.lxxxvi–vii.

23 10/4, Pt. 2.

24 *Ibid.*

25 E.g. endorsements on 2/2/134; 12/93, 143, 186, 221; 27/119.

26 3/9/94.

27 Of 139 Wolsey cases in which the form of process issued is stated, in 96 the defendants were summoned by writ of *subpoena*.

28 Returned Henrician writs of *subpoena* survive amongst the unsorted miscellaneous sacks labelled 'Chancery and Prerogative Loose Writs'; for examples of the returned star chamber *subpoena ad comparendum* from 1 Mary and 1 & 2 Philip and Mary onwards, see 10/20, Pts. 1–2. In chancery, the *quibusdam certis de causis* under the great seal was the only original process, and was there known as the *subpoena ad respondendum*. Examples are extant in

class C 253.

29 E.g. *Meggis* v. *Tretherff*, 2/18/319, 27/157.

30 See the list of appearances in 2/1/183–6.

31 E.g. *Beilby* v. *Jakson*, 2/4/40; *Fermor* v. *Newman*, 15/42–3; *Fox* v. *Fox*, 15/267; *Goldthorpp* v. *Beamond*, 18/4, 188, 25/120.

32 E.g. *Cole* v. *Thomas*, 2/10/111; *Fenton* v. *Hert*, 20/293; *Abbot of Furness* v. *Tunstall*, 15/281–2; *Hagge* v. *Bradshawe*, 33/13; *Owen* v. *Stert*, 31/167; *Warner* v. *Praty*, 28/108; *Waterton* v. *Leke*, 26/201.

33 SP 1/34, fos.5–8 (*LP* iv. 1115); Lansdowne 639, fo.25v.; 10/4, Pt. 5, fo.21; Bayne, p.clxxiv and n. 3.

34 Lansdowne 639, fo.46v.; E1 2652, fo.8v.

35 10/4, Pt. 2, *passim*; E1 2652, fo.8; Lansdowne 639, fos.25v., 26.

36 E.g. 2/33/43.

37 2/13/30–46; E1 2652, fo.1v.; E 405/75, m.3.

38 Lansdowne 639, fo.58.

39 10/4, Pt. 5, fo.9.

40 E.g. 10/4, Pt. 2; Lansdowne 639, fos. 26, 30v., 58.

41 Hargrave 216, fo.130.

42 *Ibid.*, fo. 136.

43 C 244/160/14.

44 10/4, Pt. 2; Lansdowne 639, fo.24.

45 *Benger* v. *Mexborne*, 2/4/98–108, 23/252.

46 2/23/252.

47 Lansdowne 639, fo.58.

48 *Ibid.*, fo.57v.

49 *Ibid.*, fos.23v., 27; Bayne, p.lxxxix.

50 10/4, Pt. 2.

51 *Ibid.*

52 *Dobbyns* v. *Morton*, 12/221–4; *Wyndover* v. *Kenaston*, 26/461, 17/126; Bayne, p.xcvi.

53 *Sulgrave* v. *Smythe*, 1/1/43; E1 2652, fo.11.

54 *Fenymere* v. *Waller*, 2/15/40, 24/25.

55 E1 2680.

56 Bayne, p.xcvi and references cited.

57 *Ibid.*

58 *Willoughby* v. *Jenny*, 2/17/134, 21/82, 23/121, 196.

59 *Lawrenge* v. *Huntley*, 2/18/38, 276.

60 *Kelke* v. *Gyrlyngton*, 2/23/66, 22/276, 20/363, 24/153.

61 *Sweteman* v. *Brereton*, 2/3/311, 17/227, 185, 18/162, 19/81, 22/113, 24/434, 26/370.

62 *Howard* v. *Boner*, 2/21/33.

63 Lansdowne 639, fo.27v.
64 *Ibid.*, fos.38v., 47v., 48v.
65 E1 2652, fo.11.
66 E.g. 10/4, Pt. 2.
67 Lansdowne 639, fos.26, 28.
68 Hargrave 216, fo.130.
69 *Straunge* v. *Raby*, 2/25/334; 10/4, Pt. 2.
70 *Holford* v. *Holford*, 2/24/337, 21/40; 10/4, Pt. 2.
71 Hargrave 216, fos.182v.–83.
72 10/4, Pt. 2; *Pulteney* v. *Prior of Coventry*, 2/21/56; cf. Bayne, p.xcix. For a later example, see 4/1/1.
73 *Elys* v. *Stanshawe*, 2/14/113–15; *Madely* v. *Fitzherbert*, 18/323, 25/2, 26/195, 197; Bayne, pp.civ–v.
74 E.g. 3/1/2, 20, 33, 39: 3/6/33, 106; 4/1/1, 10, 51.
75 Lansdowne 639, fos.25 (twice), 25v., 28v., 29v., 30v.; E1 2652, fo.3v.
76 Lansdowne 639, fos.24, 26v., 27, 27v. (twice), 33v. (twice); 10/4, Pt. 2.
77 E1 2652, fo.3v.; Lansdowne 639, fo.58v.
78 Lansdowne 639, fo.58; E1 2652, fo.3v.; Hargrave 216, fo.130.
79 2/20/175.
80 As n. 61 *supra*.
81 C 244/164/18A, 173/19B; SP 1/234, Pt. 1, fo.66 (*LP Add.* 422); 2/9/186, 20/164.
82 C 244/164/40, 171/22; 10/4, Pt. 5, fo.21 (twice); 2/31/fragments; 10/4, Pt. 2; Lansdowne 639, fos.25, 25v., 28v., 30.
83 C 244/171/16B; 2/17/406.
84 C 244/165/5, 166/25.
85 C 244/162/104B, 164/36, 38, 50, 165/1B, 172/42B; 2/9/186.
86 C 244/169/19.
87 Lansdowne 639, fo.53v.; E1 2652, fo.4.
88 2/17/406.
89 10/4, Pt. 5, fo.21; Lansdowne 639, fo.57.
90 West, p.195.
91 *Ibid.*
92 E.g. *Swan* v. *Smyth*, 2/32/88.
93 Bodleian, Tanner MS. 101, fo.62.
94 *Anable* v. *Starkey*, 10/4, Pt. 2.
95 Bayne, pp.civ–v. Material not available for public inspection at the time of Bayne's research confirms his account: 10/4, Pts.

1–10 (bundles); 10/8 (bundle).
96 *Booth* v. *Davenport*, 2/5/135, 164–5; *Lawrenge* v. *Huntley*, 18/38, 276; *Sweteman* v. *Brereton*, 3/311, 17/227, 185, 18/162, 19/81, 22/113, 24/434, 26/370.
97 Lansdowne 639, fos.25v., 38v.; 10/4, Pt. 2.
98 *Tyrrell* v. *Wiseman* 2/18/16, 23/222, 29/fragments; 10/4, Pt. 2; E1 2652, fo.11.
99 E1 2652, fo.16v.; 2/31/fragments, 32/fragments; 2/8/49–50, 21/45; *supra*, pp.38–9.
100 *Willoughby* v. *Willoughby*, 2/18/182, 21/17, 22–3; 10/4, Pt. 2.
101 E1 2652, fo.16v.
102 Lansdowne 639, fo.8v.
103 Only thirty-eight sets of depositions taken by commission have survived for Wolsey's chancellorship.
104 *Ardern* v. *Willoughby*, 2/2/18–23, 24/411; *Legh* v. *Massy*, 21/197; *Isot* v. *Carmynowe*, 19/196; *Ap John Gruff* v. *Gryffith*, 33/44; *Tredeneck* v. *Hamley*, 18/76, 26/242; *Pigot* v. *Giggeney*, 34/115; *Lewes* v. *Trentham*, 21/199, 200, 235.
105 E.g. 2/2/19.
106 As n. 104 *supra*.
107 10/4, Pt. 2.
108 *Ibid.*; cf. Bayne, p.cvii.
109 *Gild of Our Lady of Boston* v. *Reed*, 10/4, Pt. 3, fo.1; 2/22/39, 20/77, 19/90; *Fesaunte* v. *Gildon*, 15/67–72; *Inhabitants of Bungay* v. *Wharton*, 7/194, 26/456.
110 E1 2652, fo.16v.
111 2/4/98–108; 16/192. Bayne, pp.cvii–viii.
112 *Supra*, pp.38–9.
113 E1 2652, fos.8v., 14v.
114 E1 2655, fo.12.
115 10/4, Pt. 2; *Randell* v. *Mortymer*, 2/32/fragment; *Dallowe* v. *Pygott*, 12/46–65, 19/78, 17/386; *Earl of Northumberland* v. *Perrot*, 18/332, 27/119, 148; E1 2652, fo.10.
116 2/20/220, 13/183–6, 178–81, 29/160, 17/398.
117 *Love* v. *Maidford*, 1/1/15, 2/20/9; *Collins* v. *Wagge*, 2/10/136–36A, 24/419; Lansdowne 639, fo.24v.
118 *Eland* v. *Savell* 2/19/130, 360, 14/45–6; *Ap Gruff* v. *Ap Rice*, 17/403, 16/335–8; *Wentworth's case*, 19/239, 290, 317, 320, 336, 20/16, 43–5, 86, 128, 133, 139, 141, 24/41, 48, 147, 31/fragments; E1 2652, fo.10.
119 *Grover* v. *Lake*, 2/16/333–4, 18/125, 25/143; 10/4, Pt. 2; *Perrot* v.

Earl of Northumberland, 2/22/302; *Swift* v. *Stanley,* 10/4, Pt. 2; n. 121 *infra.*
120 *Ibid.*
121 2/27/81; 10/4, Pt. 2.
122 *Ibid.*
123 Baldwin, *King's Council,* pp.294–5.
124 The Latin reads: *'alias ago, alias audio, alias arbiter finio, alias iudex dirimo'. The Complete Works of St. Thomas More,* iv, ed. E. Surtz and J. H. Hexter (New Haven, 1965), 38. I owe this reference to Dr E. W. Ives, to whom I am in debt for a most helpful discussion of the problems of mediation and settlement in the early Tudor period. On 'umpires', see *LP* iv. 6137.
125 *Letters and Papers of John Shillingford,* ed. S. A. Moore (London, Camden Society, 1871), 41–2, 50–1, 69–70, 135–6. I owe this reference also to Dr Ives.
126 West, pp. 167–8 (especially § 44), and Year Book references cited there.
127 E.g. C 244/162/89B; 163, *passim.*
128 E.g. C 244/163/93B, 101B, 112B; 165/35; 166/25, 52A–B, 53, 56; REQ 2/2/67.
129 *Ibid.*
130 C 244/163, *passim.*
131 2/21/242; 10/4, Pt. 2.
132 2/21/242.
133 SP 1/45, fo.311 (*LP* iv. 3719).
134 2/17/24.
135 *Ibid.*
136 SP 1/42, fos. 61–4 (*LP* iv. 3154); 2/19/9, 304, 21/167, 182, 22/264.
137 2/19/304.
138 10/4, Pt. 2.
139 2/24/130, 29/fragments.
140 SP 1/234, fo.67 (*LP Add.* 422).
141 10/4, Pt. 2.
142 2/24/130.
143 *Ibid.*
144 *Ibid.*
145 10/4, Pt. 2.
146 SP 1/46, fo.252 (*LP* iv. 3926).
147 *Supra,* pp.47–9.
148 E.g. 2/32/70; Leadam, *Star Chamber 1509–1544,* pp. 25–7, 34–6.

149 *Ibid.*

150 E.g. *Frebody* v. *Assheburneham,* 2/15/304–6; *Heselerton* v. *Heselerton,* 30/139.

151 10/4, Pt. 2.

152 SP 1/46, fo.252 (*LP* iv. 3926).

153 For a similar view of the Elizabethan chancery, see Jones, p.272.

154 *Durdant* v. *Holborn,* 2/13/150–4, 156–70.

155 Such an instance occurred, though, in *Brambill* v. *Barre,* 2/29/64.

156 E.g. *Hampton* v. *Abbot of Abingdon,* 2/23/238; *Alyson* v. *Roose,* 2/1/136, 141–7.

157 E.g. *Jakson* v. *Grymston,* 2/31/170; *Carter* v. *Corrant,* REQ 3/5.

158 *Jenyn* v. *Lynche,* 2/23/72.

159 E.g. *Selby* v. *Mulsho,* 2/32/70; *Cowley* v. *Eccleston,* 2/10/301–5; *Gentilman* v. *Anderton,* 2/16/39–42; *Markenfelde* v. *Tennand,* 2/23/254; *Slak* v. *Colisen,* REQ 3/5.

160 2/19/351.

161 E.g. *Burrowe* v. *Whitefeld,* 2/7/207–8; *Smyth* v. *Sampson,* 2/22/314.

162 The story is reported in a letter from Edmund Knightley to the bench at the white hall; P.R.O., Exchequer K.R., Miscellanea B (unsorted).

163 A. J. Eagleston, *The Channel Islands under Tudor Government, 1485–1642* (Cambridge, Guernsey Society, 1949), 22–5; 2/13/135, 22/235.

164 Endorsement on *Meyre* v. *Mitton,* REQ 3/10 (visible under ultra-violet light).

165 *Fraunces* v. *Sesson,* 2/15/296–300, 26/122, 417, 29/*fragments.*

166 *Steyninges* v. *Steyninges,* 10/4, Pt. 2; 2/1/39.

167 E 315/313A, fos.43v.–44; 2/21/125, 17/172; E1 2652, fo.6; Lansdowne 639, fo.56v.

168 Cf. his statement as reported in 2/4/244.

169 2/2/159.

170 Corpus Christi College, Oxford, MS. 196, pp. 116–18.

171 Several such notes and drafts are scattered through 10/4, Pts. 2, 4.

172 2/27/81, 18/38, 276, 7/17.

173 Lansdowne 160, fo.311.

174 Guy, in *Journ. Soc. Archivists,* v. (1975), 174; cf. the clerk's note that decrees were 'entered' on 2/27/81, 23/252, 29/*fragments.*

175 The point was first made by G. R. Elton, *The Tudor Constitution* (Cambridge, 1962), 168; he rightly added, however, that the form was not typical.

176 2/5/51.

177 10/18, miscellany B/2.

178 2/21/232, 23/252, 29/fragments.

179 2/35/21.

180 E 208/19 (dated 6 November 1518).

181 2/24/130.

182 2/5/51.

183 For costs, pp.114–15 *infra*.

184 *Bowet* v. *Hall*, 2/5/149–50, 167–8, 4/228, 24/180, 19/124; *Holdforth* v. *Holdforth*, 2/21/40, 24/337, 26/82; *Plantagenet* v. *Cobley*, 2/10/66–7, 23/166, 10/65; *Carmynowe* v. *Tregian*, 2/8/134–5, 9/45, 23/239; *Hille* v. *Beale*, 2/18/192, 19/5; *Barney* v. *Sturges*, 2/33/68.

185 *Tunstall* v. *Sterky*, 2/30/126; *Blundell* v. *Molyneux*, 2/5/51; *Dowdyng* v. *Condorowe*, 2/13/30–46; *Willoughby* v. *Willoughby*, 2/17/399; *A Maryk* v. *Cave*, 2/1/150; 10/4, Pt. 2.

186 *Ganth* v. *Abbot of Whitby*, 2/16/17–18; SP 1/236, fos.45–6 (*LP Add.* 624).

187 Harleian 2143, fo.69v.; Lansdowne 639, fo.55; E1 2652, fo.9v.; E1 2655, fo.13; E1 2659.

188 E1 479; Lansdowne 639, fo.48v.

189 E1 2652, fo.11; E1 2655, fo.13; Lansdowne 639, fo.26v.

190 *Supra*, p.51.

191 *Typlary* v. *Morehouse*, 2/18/15; *Wore* v. *Berston*, 2/31/104.

192 2/1/68, 97.

193 Jones, p.314.

194 *Gyttyns* v. *Trentham*, 2/16/57–62, 425–37, 20/8.

195 This statement is based on voluntary signatures by counsel on pleadings and on the names minuted by the clerk of the council in 10/4, Pt. 2.

196 *Ibid.*; E. Foss, *Judges of England* v. (London, 1848–64), 102–3, 303; *Register of Admissions to the Honourable Society of Middle Temple* (London, 1949), i.3; Leadam, *Star Chamber 1509–1544*, pp.197–9.

197 E1 2652, fo.3v.

198 *Supra*, p.89.

199 2/17/397; 10/4, Pt. 2.

200 *Ibid.*; 2/44/155.

201 2/44/155.

202 E1 2680.

203 E1 2676.

204 Endorsements on pleadings; 3/6/106.

205 By 1600, two years were required; E1 1756.
206 *Supra,* p.69.
207 *Infra,* pp.128–30.
208 *Inhabitants of Gower* v. *Cradock,* 2/16/190–6. The case was heard in Trinity term 1524.
209 Cf. Jones' remarks on chancery, pp.306–7.
210 *Booth* v *Davenport,* 2/5/135, 164–5, 27/fragments.
211 *Rokeby* v. *Constable,* 2/29/44; E1 2652, fo.13; SP 1/34, fos.5–8 (*LP* iv 1115); Lansdowne 639, fos.56v.–57.
212 Eg. *Willoughby* v. *Jenny,* 2/17/134, 21/82, 23/121, 196; *Cod* v. *Pomell,* 2/10/69, 69A, 26/112, 32/48.
213 E.g. *Lawrenge* v. *Huntley,* 2/18/38, 276; 10/4, Pt. 2.
214 2/12/85; 10/4, Pt. 2.
215 10/4, Pt. 2.
216 2/33/43, 13/30–46, 20/172, 14/188–9, 24/404, 8/275, 31/fragments, 15/96, 8/231–2; 10/4, Pt. 2; SP 1/233, fo.274 (*LP Add.* 402).
217 *Ibid.*
218 2/13/33, 33/43.
219 SP 1/233, fo.274.
220 E1 2680.
221 2/24/404.
222 *Ibid.*
223 *Ibid.*
224 As n. 219 *supra.*
225 2/13/30–46, 8/229–32; 10/4, Pt. 2.
226 2/13/135.
227 Lansdowne 639, fo.49.
228 Harleian 2143, fo.69v.; E1 2652, fos.5, 9v.; Lansdowne 639, fos.58, 69v.; E1 2757.
229 E1 2652, fo.5.
230 As n. 219 *supra.*
231 10/4, Pt. 10.
232 Harleian 2143, fo.69v. The correct date is established by E1 2652, fo.12.
233 *Ibid.*
234 E1 2757.
235 2/25/214; SP 1/17, fos.248–9 (*LP* ii. App. 60); E 36/215, fo.347; E 36/216, fos. 172, 176; E 401/958.
236 SP 1/17, fos. 248–9; E1 2652, fo.8v.
237 2/25/214; *LP* ii. 3752.

238 C 244/165/1B.
239 C 54/386; E 36/216, fo.176.
240 C 54/386.
241 CP 40/1022, *roti.* 548, 739.
242 E1 2652, fo.8v.; 2/25/214.
243 E 36/125, fos.13v., 25; E 401/958; E 405/78, m.37; SP 1/67, fo.33v. (printed in Elton, *Tudor Revolution,* pp. 434–5).
244 E 137/143/2.
245 Cf. Bayne, p. clxxi.
246 E 36/216, fo.176; E 101/414/16, fo.214; SP 1/16, fos.35–6 (*LP* ii. 3741); C 244/168/15A.
247 E.g. *LP* ii. 3752.
248 Lansdowne 639, fo.48v.
249 C 244/165/1B.
250 Bayne, p. clxxiv.
251 E1 2652, fo.8v.; 2/15/116.
252 E1 2652, fos.8v., 14v.; Lansdowne 639, fo.47.
253 E1 479; E1 2652, fo.14v.; Lansdowne 639, fos.47v., 49, 56.
254 E1 2652, fo.14.
255 E1 2655, fo.14v.

CHAPTER 5

1 *Supra,* pp.27, 31.
2 B.M. Cotton MS. Titus B. i, fo.183.
3 E1 2655, fo.15v.
4 E.g. C 254/161/25–6.
5 C 254/161/26.
6 *Tudor Royal Proclamations,* i.153–4.
7 E1 2652, fo.12.
8 J. H. Langbein, *Prosecuting Crime in the Renaissance: England, Germany, France* (Cambridge, Mass., 1974), 34–5, 104–5.
9 *Tudor Royal Proclamations,* i.172–4; *supra,* p.70.
10 *LP* iv. 3664, 3702–3.
11 *LP* iv. 3664, 3702.
12 E.g. *LP* iv. 3665, 3712, 3822.
13 *LP* iv. 3869 (29), 3991 (3).
14 R. B. Smith, *Land and Politics in the England of Henry VIII: the West Riding of Yorkshire* (Oxford, 1970), 153–5.

15 *Ibid.;* B.M. Cotton MS. Titus B. i, fos.295–7.
16 Smith, p.145; *St. Pap.,* iv. 155.
17 C. Haigh, *Reformation and Resistance in Tudor Lancashire* (Cambridge, 1975), 105.
18 *Ibid.,* SP 1/23, fos.228–31 (*LP* iii. 1923 [2]).
19 Smith, pp.142–3.
20 SP 1/51, fos.288–92 (*LP* iv. 5107); *LP* iv. 5954; Pollard, p.319.
21 Pollard, p.319.
22 2/24/79.
23 *Tudor Royal Proclamations,* i.143–4.
24 *Ibid.*
25 *St. Pap.,* iv. 155. Cf. the report of the previous year, discussed in R. R. Reid, *The King's Council in the North* (London, 1921), 95–6.
26 Reid, p.93 n. 2.
27 *St. Pap.,* iv. 155, 242.
28 E1 2652, fo.6; Lansdowne 1, fo.105.
29 C 244/168/15A; *LP* iv. 3022.
30 Reid, pp.93–4.
31 *St. Pap.,* iv. 54.
32 *St. Pap.,* iv. 420.
33 *LP* iv. 4790.
34 Fully described by Dr Reid (pp.102–12), who concludes that, despite other setbacks, the judicial work of the council was successful, not least as a fully-fledged criminal court empowered by commission of *oyer et terminer.*
35 Pollard, pp.72–80.
36 *Studies in Tudor and Stuart Politics and Government* (Cambridge, 1974), i. 118.
37 2/3/244–6, 19/375, 20/340; 10/1/41.
38 2/1/23.
39 2/26/426; 10/4, Pt. 2, which establishes the correct date.
40 Endorsed on the plaintiff's bill.
41 DL 3/11/B5.
42 DL 3/11/B6.
43 *Ibid.*
44 2/5/49–51.
45 SP 1/45, fo.51 (*LP* iv. 3579); 2/24/181, 29/86.
46 2/15/117.
47 *The Complete Peerage,* ed. G. E. Cokayne (London, 1896), vii.157.
48 2/15/114, 117.
49 D. W. Sutherland, *The Assize of Novel Disseisin* (Oxford, 1973),

192–3.
50 2/15/117.
51 2/15/117–18.
52 2/15/109.
53 2/20/315.
54 Endorsement on 2/20/315.
55 2/15/114–15.
56 2/15/116; E1 2655, fo.13.
57 *Ibid.*
58 2/15/111.
59 2/13/121.
60 2/15/109; SP 60/1, fo.98 (*LP* iv. 2076).
61 By 4 Hen. VII, c.17.
62 2/20/347.
63 2/15/109.
64 *Ibid.*; Sutherland, p.170.
65 2/15/109.
66 2/20/347.
67 C 142/55/25.
68 Mainly inquisitions *post mortem,* especially C 142/125/24, 180/28.
69 E.g. endorsements on pleadings in REQ 3/3–10.
70 E. W. Ives, 'The Common Lawyers in Pre-Reformation England', *Transactions of the Royal Historical Society,* 5th series, xviii (1968), 165–70.
71 *Ibid.,* p.165.
72 *Supra,* p.45.
73 E.g. Ives, p.170; *LP* iv. 5750, 6075; 'Replication of a Sergeant at the Laws of England', in *Doctor and Student,* ed. W. Muchall (London, 1815), especially p.7.
74 Ives, p.171.
75 Lansdowne 1, fo. 108v.; *LP* iv. 6019; Pollard, p.255.
76 *LP* iv. 6025.
77 Elton, *Studies,* i.152, 155–7, 170–2, 177–88.
78 *Ibid.,* i.152–3; *LP* iv. 6043 (1).
79 Elton, *Studies,* i.171–2.
80 *Ibid.,* i.172, 185–6.
81 21 Hen. VIII, c.20.
82 2/20/223.
83 Pollard, pp.255–6.
84 *LP* iv. 6019, 6030.

85 Suffolk had been excluded by Wolsey; El 2655, fo.10v.

86 A. F. Pollard, 'Council, Star Chamber, and Privy Council under the Tudors', *E.H.R.*, xxxvii (1922), 353–4.

87 He retained the style, however, for some years.

88 Elton, *Studies*, i.172.

89 Lansdowne 1, fo.108v.

90 Roper's story that More read through bills of complaint himself and authorised the issue of writs of *subpoena* by his own signature is partly confirmed by the records. Other lord chancellors had no time for this personal scrutiny. *The Lyfe of Sir Thomas Moore*, ed. E. V. Hitchcock (London, Early English Text Society, 1935), 43.

91 Professor Margaret Hastings is currently at work on More as a judge.

92 10/4, Pt. 2.

93 Lansdowne 639, fo.22.

94 10/4, Pt. 2; 2/17/405.

95 Elton, *Tudor Revolution*, pp.321–2, 324.

96 Cf. Elton, *Studies*, i.172.

97 *Ibid.*, i.186–7.

98 As it had on one occasion in 1511; Lansdowne 639, fo. 40v.

99 *LP* v. 1472.

100 Elton, *Tudor Revolution*, pp.334–5.

101 El 2652, fo.4v.

102 Elton, *Tudor Revolution*, pp.334–43; *Trans. Roy. Hist. Soc.*, 5th series, xxv (1975), 201–2.

103 Elton, *Tudor Constitution*, pp.90–1, 95.

104 Corpus Christi College, Oxford, MS.196, fos.116–23.

105 Elton, *Tudor Revolution*, p.344.

106 *LP* vi. 1381 (3).

107 *Ibid.*, no. 11.

108 *Ibid.*, no. 10; G. R. Elton, *Reform and Renewal* (Cambridge, 1973), 142.

109 SP 1/101, fos.311–12 (*LP* x. 246 [6]), the relevant passage being printed in W. S. Holdsworth, *A History of English Law*, iv (London, 1924), p.584 § 9. *LP* xiii, App.5.

110 E.g. 2/2/183–7, 190–3; *LP* viii. 457.

111 *LP* xiii, App.5.

112 C 115/M20.

113 Elton, *Reform and Renewal*, p.24.

114 *Ibid.*, p.142.

115 *Ibid.*, p.141; C 66/664, m.33 (misleadingly calendared in *LP* vii.

1601 [33]).

116 Elton, *Studies*, i.331 n.2.

117 Elton, *Reform and Renewal*, p.24.

118 A bibliography of the *Reports* is being prepared by Professor T. G. Barnes, who is also writing the history of star chamber from 1596 to 1641.

119 C.U.L., MS Ii. 6. 51, fo.51 (Layton's case).

120 *De Republica Anglorum*, ed. L. Alston (Cambridge, 1906), 118.

List of Primary Sources

The following are the principal manuscripts on which this study has been based. For other references to documents in the P.R.O., the footnotes should be consulted.

Public Record Office
STAC 1/1–2
STAC 2/ 1–35
STAC 3/1–9
STAC 4/1–11
STAC 10/1–21 (under arrangement)
C 44/36–37B (under arrangement)
C 54/383–98
C 66/624–55
C 193/1–3
C 244/159–72
C 253/53–56
C 254/158–62
E 28/93–96
E 36/124–25, 194, 215–16
E 101/414/16, 517/11
E 137/143/2
E 163/9/20, 24/9
E 208/19
E 315/313A

E 407/51–55
REQ 1/1–5, 104–5
REQ 3/1–38 (under arrangement)
SP 1/1–60, 231–46
SP 2/Λ

British Museum
Additional MSS. 4520–21, 5485, 11681, 21480–81, 24926, 26647, 28201, 36111–12, 41661.
Cotton MSS. Titus B.i, B.iv–v; Vespasian C.xiv; Vespasian F.ix, F.xiii.
Hargrave MSS. 216, 237, 250–51, 290, 482.
Harleian MSS. 297, 305, 425, 444, 736, 829, 859, 1200, 1226, 1576, 1689, 2143, 3504, 4272, 4274, 5350, 6235, 6256, 6448, 6811, 6815, 7161.
Lansdowne MSS. 1, 69, 83, 160, 232, 254, 622, 639, 830, 905.
Stowe MSS. 145, 418–19.

Henry E. Huntington Library.
Ellesmere MSS. 436, 438–40, 446, 465, 479, 481, 485–86, 495, 1169, 2562, 2652–59, 2661, 2670, 2683, 2685, 2725, 2739–40, 2746, 2757, 2759, 2761, 2764–69, 2810, 7921.

Guildhall, London
MS. 1751

All Souls College, Oxford
MSS. 178A–B, 256, 258.

Bodleian Library
MSS. Carte 119, Douce 66, Eng. hist. c.304, Tanner 101.

Corpus Christi College, Oxford
MS. 196

St. Edmund Hall, Oxford
MS. 3

University Library, Cambridge
Additional MS. 3105; MSS. Dd. 11. 58, Dd. 11. 81, Gg. 5. 18, Ii. 6. 54, Kk. 6. 22, Ll. 3. 3, Ll. 4. 10, Mm. 5. 12.

Folger Shakespeare Library
MSS. V. a. 207 (formerly 511121.1), V. b. 179, V. b. 205.

INDEX

181